CHANGING PATTERNS

of U.S. Industrial Activity and Comparative Advantage

BY JOHN MUTTI
AND PETER MORICI

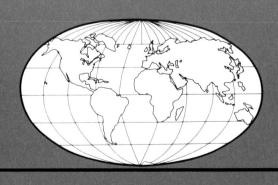

NPA Committee on
Changing International Realities

NPA's Committee on Changing International Realities and Their Implications for U.S. Policy

Profound changes have been taking place since the 1970s in the nature of the international political and economic system and in the position of the United States within it. These continuing developments involve new and highly complex kinds of interactions among nations. In consequence, many of the assumptions about international economic and political relationships that were relevant during the 1950s and '60s can no longer serve as valid bases for governmental and private policymaking. Today and for the future, policymakers need new concepts and data relevant to the changing realities of the present period if they are to serve the interests of the United States and the welfare of the American people. And, because the United States has a predominantly private enterprise economy, policies affecting the ability of the U.S. private sector to function effectively both at home and abroad are of crucial importance for realizing these national goals.

Accordingly, in 1975, NPA established the Committee on Changing International Realities and Their Implications for U.S. Policy (CIR) to undertake a continuing two-part program. It consists of (1) research on the nature and probable future development of the new international realities and of U.S. capabilities and needs relative to them, and (2) based on these analyses and forecasts, suggestions for governmental and private policies to improve the international performance of the U.S. economy so that it can better protect and advance the interests of the United States and the well-being of the American people.

In accordance with NPA's practice, the CIR consists of experienced leaders from the main private-sector groups: business corporations and banks, labor unions, farm organizations, and the professions. The Committee meets twice a year to discuss subjects to be researched, to review outlines and drafts of studies under way and to consider their policy implications. Detailed guidance of the CIR's research program is carried on by subcommittees concerned with various subject areas. Professional and administrative staff services are provided to the Committee under the supervision of the Director of NPA's International Division.

For information about the CIR or NPA's other committee and research activities, please get in touch with:

Laura Megna Baughman
NPA Director of Public Affairs

National Planning Association
1606 New Hampshire Avenue, N.W.
Washington, D.C. 20009
(202) 265–7685

A description of NPA as a whole and a list of its Officers and Board of Trustees are printed at the end of this publication.

CHANGING PATTERNS

of U.S. Industrial Activity and Comparative Advantage

BY JOHN MUTTI
University of Wyoming

AND PETER MORICI
National Planning Association

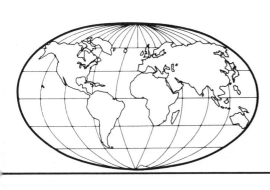

NPA Committee on
Changing International Realities

Changing Patterns of U.S. Industrial Activity
and Comparative Advantage

CIR Report #14
NPA Report #201

Price $8.00

ISBN 0-89068-069-8
Library of Congress
Catalog Card Number 83-62893

 C 439

Contents

**Changing Patterns of U.S. Industrial
Activity and Comparative Advantage**

by John Mutti and Peter Morici

	NPA's Committee on Changing International Realities and Their Implications for U.S. Policy	*inside front cover*
	A Statement by the Committee	v
	Members of the Committee Signing the Statement	vii
	PART ONE	
Chapter 1	**Overview of the Issues**	1
Chapter 2	**Measuring and Interpreting Changing Industry Structure and Competitiveness**	5
	Alternative Measures of Industry Structure and Competitiveness	5
	Determinants of Industry Structure and Competitiveness	6
	Trends among Industrial Countries	7
	Trends in the NICs	10
	Other Structural Considerations	10
	Summary	11
Chapter 3	**Trends in Industry Structure and Competitiveness— an Aggregate View**	12
	Trends in Industrial Structure	12
	Trends in International Competitiveness	16
Chapter 4	**Trends within Manufacturing**	20
	Industry Characteristics	22
	Comparisons of Changing International Competitiveness and Industry Structure	24
	Changes in the AICs as a Group	30
	Changes in the Individual AICs	31
	Conclusions	34
	PART TWO	
Chapter 5	**The Role of Government Policies**	37
	General Aspects of Government Policies	37
	Country Surveys	38
	Japan	38
	Germany	41
	United Kingdom	42
	France	44
	Canada	45
	Conclusions	47

| Chapter 6 | **Issues Facing the United States** | **49** |

Issues Facing the United States 49
A Selective Survey of U.S. Policies 50
Alternative Policy Approaches 53
Market-oriented Approach 53
Improved Limited Intervention 54
Industrial Policy Planning 56
Conclusions 58

Selected Bibliography 60

National Planning Association 61

NPA Officers and Board of Trustees 62

Recent NPA Publications *inside back cover*

Tables

1. Income Elasticities of Demand for Selected Categories of Personal Consumption Expenditure, United States 6

2. Relative Resource Endowments, 1963 and 1980 8

3. Rates of Resource Growth, 1963–80, Relative to Total Labor Force 9

4. Changing Patterns of Production in Selected AICs 13

5. Annual Growth Rates of Real Output in Selected AICs, 1960–79 14

6. Changing Structure of International Trade, 1973 and 1979 15

7. U.S. Industry Input Characteristics, 1979 23

8. Changes in International Competitiveness, Export-Import Ratios
United States 25
Japan 25
Germany 26
United Kingdom 26
Canada 27

9. Changes in Industrial Structure, Industry Shares of Total Manufacturing Value Added
United States 27
Japan 28
Germany 28
United Kingdom 29
Canada 29

10. Summary of Changes in International Competitiveness and Industry Structure 30

A Statement by the Committee on Changing International Realities

Since its founding in 1975, the Committee on Changing International Realities has been concerned with the ever more intense competition faced by American industry in international markets. The growth of import penetration in a succession of established manufacturing sectors, such as textiles and apparel, footwear, consumer electronics, steel, and automobiles, as well as the increased challenge to U.S. leadership in high technology activities at home and in export markets, make the long-term competitive viability of U.S. industry one of the most critical public policy issues of this decade. Indeed, as industrialization in Latin America and Asia continues to spread and diversify, and other advanced industrialized countries place greater emphasis on technology-intensive activities, competitive pressures on U.S. firms and workers will likely intensify rather than abate. And with the United States increasingly involved in international markets, the competitive viability of U.S. industry is critical to achieving high levels of employment and secure and rising standards of living. Consequently, the Committee on Changing International Realities (CIR) continues to seek to play a constructive role through the publication of *Changing Patterns of U.S. Industrial Activity and Comparative Advantage* by John Mutti and Peter Morici, the seventh in its series of studies on U.S. competitiveness.

In recent years, public policymakers, opinion leaders and scholars have become increasingly concerned about the roles of domestic and international macroeconomic policies pursued by the United States and its major trading partners and exchange rates in determining patterns of trade and international competitiveness. As tariffs have been reduced through successive rounds of GATT-sponsored negotiations, attention has in addition increasingly turned to the industrial policies pursued by U.S. trading partners designed to protect or promote their import-competing and export-oriented activities. Concern has emerged that some of these policies are exerting significant influence on the trade performance of U.S. industries. These concerns, coupled with the difficult structural adjustments now under way in the American economy, have given rise to a national debate on how U.S. policies can best be framed to help U.S. industry be more competitive.

In this study, the authors analyze recent changes in underlying structural conditions — e.g., the availability of capital, various kinds of skilled labor and R&D capabilities — in the United States, Japan, Germany, the United Kingdom, France, and Canada. In addition, they examine changes in these six industrialized countries' competitive performance in three major sectors (agriculture, mining and manufacturing) and 20 individual manufacturing industries, with particular emphasis on three types of activities — labor-intensive, capital-intensive producing standardized goods, and technology-intensive. Finally, they analyze the general thrust and orientation of the industrial policies pursued by these countries and assess the ways in which these domestic and international economic policies may be influencing their international competitive performances.

The authors conclude that much of the recent changes in the six industrialized countries' competitive performance is consistent with changes in the availability of capital, in various types of labor and in R&D capabilities. However, they find evidence that industrial policies are influential as well. For example, their analysis indicates that government efforts to reorient the Japanese economy away from heavy industries toward technology-intensive activities have been successful in increasing the vulnerability of U.S. and European producers to Japanese competition in these areas. In contrast, the authors find that policies pursued in the United Kingdom may have had the opposite effects.

As never before, national debate includes not only macroeconomic policy questions but also the appropriate role for government policy in assisting U.S. firms and workers to achieve improved international competitiveness. At this point, therefore, we believe it urgent to undertake careful evaluations of U.S. underlying structural conditions and of industrial policies at home and abroad that influence the potential for better competitive performance.

In our view, this report is such an evaluation. The data and analysis it presents should promote better understanding of the important domestic and international economic policy issues of the day and deserve the attention of private- and public-sector decisionmakers and concerned citizens.

Accordingly, regardless of whether we, as individuals, agree or disagree with all of the study's specific interpretations and conclusions, we believe it makes an important and timely contribution to the understanding of vital economic policy questions confronting the nation. Therefore, we are pleased to recommend that it be published by NPA as a report signed by the authors.

Members of the Committee on Changing International Realities Signing the Statement

CHARLES E. MCKITTRICK, JR.
Vice President, Governmental Programs, IBM

JOHN MILLER
Vice Chairman, National Planning Association

WILLIAM R. MILLER
President, Pharmaceutical and Nutritional Group,
Bristol-Myers Company

ALFRED F. MIOSSI
Executive Vice President, Continental Illinois
National Bank & Trust Company of Chicago

WILLIAM R. PEARCE
Corporate Vice President, Cargill Incorporated

RALPH A. PFEIFFER, JR.
Chairman of the Board and Chief Executive Officer,
World Trade Americas, Far East Corp., IBM

MYER RASHISH
President, Rashish Associates, Inc.

JERRY REES
Executive Vice President, National Association
of Wheat Growers

WILLIAM D. ROGERS
Partner, Arnold & Porter

HERBERT SALZMAN
Westport, Connecticut

NATHANIEL SAMUELS
Advisory Director, Lehman Brothers Kuhn Loeb, Inc.

DANIEL I. SARGENT
Managing Director, Salomon Brothers, Inc.

A.C. SHEFFIELD
Group Vice President, Fluor Corporation

MARK SHEPHERD, JR.
Chairman of the Board and Chief Executive
Officer, Texas Instruments Incorporated

WINFRIED H. SPAEH
General Manager, Dresdner Bank

WILLIAM F. SPENGLER
President and Chief Operating Officer, Domestic
Operations, Owens-Illinois

ROBERT B. STEVENS
President, Haverford College

RALPH I. STRAUS
New York, New York

WALTER STERLING SURREY
Senior Partner, Surrey and Morse

ANTHONY P. TERRACCIANO
Executive Vice President and Chief Financial
Officer, The Chase Manhattan Bank, N.A.

ALEXANDER C. TOMLINSON
President, National Planning Association

THOMAS N. URBAN
President and Chief Executive Officer, Pioneer
Hi-Bred International

MARK H. WILLES
Executive Vice President and Chief Financial
Officer, General Mills, Inc.

ROBERT A. WILSON
Vice President, Public Affairs, Pfizer Inc.

ALAN WM. WOLFF
Partner, Verner, Liipfert, Bernhard & McPherson

CHARLES G. WOOTTON
Senior Director, Public Affairs, Gulf Oil Corporation

RALPH S. YOHE
Editor, *Wisconsin Agriculturalist*

The opinions expressed and the recommendations presented in the Committee Statement are solely those of the individual members of the Committee on Changing International Realities whose signatures are offered hereto and do not represent the views of the National Planning Association or its staff.

PART ONE

Overview of the Issues 1

Since World War II, the U.S. position as the economic leader of the free world has declined. As one example, the U.S. share of total world merchandise exports fell from 18 percent in 1955 to 13 percent in 1981. Over this same time period, though, exports as a share of GNP rose from less than 4 percent to 8 percent, while imports increased even more rapidly to 9 percent of GNP. Thus, while the dominance of the United States has fallen, the U.S. economy has become more closely linked to the rest of the world. As a consequence, policies that affect U.S. competitiveness internationally have become more important.

The United States emerged from World War II with a strong competitive position in a broad range of industries including many that are now threatened by import competition. With the European and Japanese industrial bases damaged, the United States became the major source of many products necessary for economic recovery. Yet, dependence on world markets for raw materials and manufactured goods was limited, and exports were not regarded as a significant source of new jobs.

Over the last three decades, however, the U.S. economy has been internationalized. Merchandise exports as a share of GNP increased steadily and, at the same time, U.S. dependence on imports of raw materials grew. U.S. international competitiveness waned in many manufacturing activities, as Japan (and later the newly industrializing countries—NICs) captured major shares of U.S. markets. Imports displaced domestic production first in low wage labor-intensive industries characterized by fairly accessible production technologies—e.g., apparel and footwear. Then, as other industries matured and their products and technologies of production became fairly standardized, Japan (followed by the NICs) also gained substantial if not dominant shares of U.S. markets—e.g., black and white (then color) televisions and other consumer electronic goods. Recently, imports have captured significant market shares in more sophisticated capital-intensive basic industries such as steel and automobiles.

As a result of these trends, the United States has come to rely more and more on exports of agricultural products, manufactures requiring highly skilled engineers and technicians, and services, as well as on the ability of U.S. firms and entrepreneurs to move into successive generations of newly emerging industries. In the years ahead, however, the U.S. export growth in agricultural products and services will continue to be constrained by substantial trade barriers, which are not effectively covered by the General Agreement on Tariffs and Trade (GATT), and in agricultural products further by the limited growth of potential markets. Meanwhile, traditionally strong U.S. export manufacturing industries face growing competition from European and Japanese producers, which are often supported by foreign government subsidies. U.S. leadership in industries such as chemicals, commercial aircraft and heavy machinery cannot be taken for granted.

Some individual industries have experienced much larger competitive pressures than average figures suggest, and the resulting patterns of unemployment have imposed significant social costs. Sectors with expanding job opportunities seldom require the same skills nor are located in the same geographic areas as contracting industries. Owners of failing businesses usually do not share in the gains of expanding industries. Often, displaced workers can only find jobs at much lower wage rates, or they give up looking for work entirely. Adjustments are not automatic or costless to individuals or society as a whole.

In an effort to cushion or postpone the adjustment process, many advanced industrial countries (AICs) have intervened to assist import-impacted industries with import restrictions and financial aid. Assistance has not been limited to import-competing industries alone; as export industries have seen their competitiveness challenged, subsidized export credits, special tax benefits and other incentives have become common throughout the Organization for Economic Cooperation and Development (OECD).

Debate over the way in which the U.S. government should respond to the rapid pace of economic change has spread to a progressively wider audience. The apparent success of certain countries, especially Japan, in selecting priority industries for expansion has prompted some to recommend a more active and systematically implemented U.S. policy. However, not all efforts to identify and promote promising industries of the future have been successful, even in Japan. Consequently, others argue for even greater reliance on market forces by the elimination of many programs and regulations already in place. Either position represents dissatisfaction with the status quo. But formulating better policies and building a national consensus behind them require general agreement about appropriate goals and a clearer understanding of the scope and causes of the shifts in industry structure and competitiveness now occurring.

For example, too often U.S. comparative advantages are described as being concentrated solely in agriculture, high technology manufacturing and sophisticated services. While these are the dominant areas of U.S. strength and the major sources of U.S. export earnings, the conclusions that special measures are necessary to promote them further or that their competitive advantage will remain constant are not justified. U.S. export potential in these areas is constrained by the depth of potential markets in agriculture and the progress achieved by the other AICs in high technology and service activities, as well as by the many artificial barriers to U.S. exports. Moreover, in recent years, U.S. competitive advantages may have improved, or at least U.S. competitive disadvantages may have been reduced in other areas, increasing the U.S. potential to achieve exports, or at least better compete with imports. The most notable example is textiles.

The purpose of this study is to identify and analyze some of the basic trends in international competitiveness and industry structure of the United States and the other AICs. The following questions will be addressed.

- To what extent do all developed countries face a similar set of competitive pressures?

- How have U.S. competitive advantages and disadvantages changed?

- How are changes in U.S. competitiveness in manufacturing related to changes in industry structure in the United States and elsewhere? In particular, have other AICs expanded their capabilities more rapidly in areas where the United States has traditionally enjoyed strength? Have other AICs' industrial structures become more similar to that of the United States, making more difficult the maintenance of U.S. competitive advantages in areas of traditional strength?

• To what extent have other countries better responded to competitive pressures by altering their industry structures more rapidly than the United States?

• What role have other AICs' government policies played in creating competitive pressures on the United States?

• What are the implications for the direction of U.S. policy?

A basic framework is developed in Chapter 2 to examine how and why the structures of industry and competitiveness have changed. The roles of demand factors—e.g., income levels—and supply variables—e.g., the availability and vintage of capital, the quality of the labor force and access to the most current technology—are analyzed.

In Chapter 3, this framework is used to survey trends in industry structure and competitiveness for the United States, Japan, Germany, the United Kingdom, France, and Canada at the aggregate level, that is, by examining broad trends in agriculture, extractive industries, manufacturing, and services over the last 20 years.

One general trend is that income growth in the AICs has resulted in a production shift toward the service sector. Over the past decade, this shift has been observed in five of the six countries studied, except in Japan. The position of the manufacturing sector and its competitiveness internationally are closely related to supply factors, such as the availability of natural resources. Relatively resource-rich countries such as Canada, the United Kingdom and the United States have seen the competitiveness of their manufacturing sectors decline over the 1970s, while relatively resource-poor countries such as Japan and France have seen their competitiveness increase.

This information provides a useful background from which to examine in Chapter 4 trends in industry structure and competitiveness in 20 disaggregated industries within the manufacturing sector. While the role of interventionist government policies cannot be denied in an examination of particular industries, shifts in underlying structural conditions are playing a principal role in determining the emerging pattern of U.S. competitiveness. The challenge to the United States and other AICs from the NICs in labor-intensive industries may be expected to continue and to expand into other manufacturing activities such as automobiles, steel and nonferrous metals. Meanwhile, major changes in the other AICs have allowed them to catch up with the United States in many capital-intensive and high technology industries. Although the United States still maintains a comparative advantage in many of these areas, it has been significantly weakened by higher rates of capital investment and greater emphasis on the training of scientists and engineers in Japan and Europe.

This survey demonstrates that the United States is not the only country facing a Japanese challenge, as the competitiveness of technology-intensive industries has fallen in Germany and the United Kingdom in spite of the more favorable pattern of factor growth conditions within those countries. The uneven nature of these competitive changes suggests that other forces, particularly government policy, have played a role in determining the competitiveness of particular industries. Therefore, the scope of government intervention is discussed in Part Two of the study.

In Chapter 5, the policies of countries outside the United States are examined. The Japanese goal of shifting its industrial structure toward technology-intensive industries has been successful and is an important reason why the rapid growth of capital in Japan has not caused comparable expansion in other industries. The rapid rise of Japanese competitiveness in technology-intensive industries has intensified the competitive pressures on European and U.S. producers.

The European response to this challenge has differed across countries. In the United Kingdom, greater attention has been paid to the declining prospects of more traditional industries such as steel. In France, the government has taken an active role in promoting many high technology industries, and the nationalistic focus adopted in the 1960s and 1970s is likely to continue under the current socialist government, in spite of its political commitments to more traditional industries. In Germany, government policies have had a more general, less project-specific focus than in Japan or France; the decline in German competitiveness in high technology industries raises the question whether its trade position has been forced on it by the policies of other countries.

Many of these issues are relevant in evaluating recent U.S. experience and policy options. The first part of Chapter 6 recounts aspects of current U.S. government policy, while the second part outlines three alternative policy approaches for the future. Discussion of these alternatives summarizes a wide range of issues confronting the United States as it formulates policies over the rest of the decade.

Measuring and Interpreting Changing Industry Structure and Competitiveness 2

A country's industrial structure evolves in response to changes in underlying demand and supply conditions. Shifts in demand conditions, resulting from changes in income levels, tastes, technology, and product design, and from the size and composition of the government sector, determine how a society allocates its expenditures on goods and services among various sectors of the economy. Within each sector, whether a larger or smaller share of these sales is accounted for by domestic or foreign firms, and whether there are substantial imports or exports, depends on the cost competitiveness of home producers relative to foreign producers. The latter depends on the availability of necessary capital, labor and natural resources, the size of the domestic market and the importance of economies of scale, and the magnitude and nature of government intervention in the market.

Measures of changes in industry structure and competitiveness are briefly discussed next, while the following section analyzes the factors affecting the evolution of industry structure and competitiveness in the United States and elsewhere.

ALTERNATIVE MEASURES OF INDUSTRY STRUCTURE AND COMPETITIVENESS

In this study, industrial structure is measured by the share of total GNP accounted for by a particular sector. These shares can be compared across countries to demonstrate, for example, whether the steel industry plays the same role in the U.S. economy as it does in the Japanese economy. When the shares for all industries in the United States are very similar to those for another country, such as the United Kingdom, the two countries are considered to have similar industrial structures.

When an industry grows faster than the economywide average, its share of GNP will increase; if its growth rate is below average, its share will decline. Therefore, the way shares of GNP change over time indicates which sectors are growing more or less rapidly and becoming more or less important.

International competitiveness is measured here primarily by the ratio of exports to imports. When the ratio is increasing, a country's competitive position is considered to be improving, since sales to foreigners have become relatively larger than purchases from foreign sources. That ratio will not be particularly distorted by worldwide inflationary trends, as would a simple trade balance (i.e., exports minus imports). Also, it is simpler to compute than commonly used ratios of exports to shipments or imports to apparent consumption. While such measures may be more desirable for some comparisons, the data necessary for international comparisons at the industry level often are not available. For the purposes of this study, all three measures yield comparable interpretations of the nature of changing international competitiveness.

DETERMINANTS OF INDUSTRY STRUCTURE AND COMPETITIVENESS

Industry structure evolves in part (as noted above) because of changes in the pattern of demand for goods produced by various sectors and industries. Some change may result from the development of new technologies and products, advertising and the diffusion of new ideas, and other trends in the market place. The effects of these changes on the growth and importance of broadly defined industrial sectors often show up only in the long run; in the short run, the important demand-side determinant is changes in income.

The effects of income growth on expenditure patterns would be neutral or proportional if a 1 percent increase in income led to a 1 percent increase in demand for all goods. The fact is, as incomes grow, expenditures on goods and services from some sectors increase much more rapidly than others. In particular, as incomes grow in affluent societies, expenditures on services expand most rapidly, while those of many goods-producing sectors grow only slowly.

Table 1 presents income elasticities for the United States. These elasticities are greater than one if a 1 percent increase in income is expected to result in more than a 1 percent increase in sales, other things remaining the same; hence, they show which sectors of the economy are likely to benefit most as incomes grow. They support the general thesis that as economies become more affluent, they

TABLE 1. INCOME ELASTICITIES OF DEMAND FOR SELECTED CATEGORIES
OF PERSONAL CONSUMPTION EXPENDITURE, UNITED STATES

	Elasticity Value
Food	
Fruits and vegetables	0.30
Meat products	0.50
Alcoholic beverages	1.40
Consumer nondurables	
Broad and narrow fabrics	0.85
Apparel	1.00
Household textiles	1.35
Leather footwear	0.70
Consumer durables	
Household appliances	1.70
Radio and TV receivers	1.70
Motor vehicles	1.00
Services	
Airlines	2.00
Telephone and telegraph	1.50
Retail trade	1.35
Credit agencies and brokers	1.45
Owner-occupied dwellings	0.45
Real estate	1.45
Hotels and lodging	1.50
Medical services	0.80
Private schools and nonprofit organizations	1.80

Source: Clopper Almon, et al., *1985: Interindustry Forecasts of the American Economy* (Lexington, Mass.: D.C. Heath, 1974), p. 37.

tend to become more service-oriented (e.g., income elasticities for services are greater than one). For many goods this elasticity is less than one. For example, if U.S. agriculture is to find expanding markets, it must seek export growth, since income expansion at home will not generate large sales increases. Also significant is the high elasticity for alcoholic beverages, indicating that high growth industries need not be strong export industries. In fact, export industries may find their competitive position weakened as input costs are driven up by the expansion of some domestically oriented sectors. Other things being equal, on the basis of these demand considerations, as incomes expand, a general increase in the importance of the service sector in the AICs can be expected as well as a decline in the share of GNP originating in agriculture, mining and manufacturing. But within the major trading sectors (agriculture, mining, manufacturing, and selected services), specialization can be expected among the AICs, and between the AICs and the rest of the world, on the basis of comparative advantage. For example, due to favorable cost conditions in Canada and the United States for agricultural commodities and natural resources, the two countries will export products intensive in the use of those resources, or at least will display more self-sufficiency.

A country's underlying cost considerations and comparative advantages are probably most dependent on the availability of various basic factors of production—physical capital, innovative capacity (R&D capital), various types of skilled labor, arable land, and natural resources. Other institutional and social factors are also important, such as entrepreneurial ability, labor management relations, incentive structures, and forms of business organizations. Although those factors cannot be measured easily, they change less rapidly over time than the availability of various types of capital and labor. Therefore, to explain changing competitiveness internationally over a 10- or 15-year period, it is essential to look at the changing availability of resources across countries.

Economists expect countries to display cost advantages in the industries that require more of their most plentiful resources. For example, economists expect countries with relatively more capital to produce capital-intensive goods more cheaply and to export some of those goods, in the absence of government intervention. And if a country is abundant in capital, but chooses to save and invest less than other nations, it can expect its cost advantage, and hence its competitive position, to erode.

Trends among Industrial Countries

For 1963 and 1980, Table 2 shows the resource shares of capital, various types of labor, arable land, and R&D scientists and engineers for six major AICs and six NICs. Reading across any line, a higher value indicates greater relative abundance for that factor.

The *United States* enjoys a comparative advantage among the AICs in goods and services that require more scientific know-how and more physical capital. But from 1963 to 1980, the U.S. share of those resources dropped particularly rapidly; hence, the U.S. advantage in R&D-oriented and capital-intensive industries should decline compared to the other AICs, especially Japan. However, the U.S. competitive advantage in these areas, while weakened, should not disappear.

These trends are attributable to the lower rates of savings and capital formation in the United States and the stronger efforts to increase the supply of and

TABLE 2. RELATIVE RESOURCE ENDOWMENTS, 1963 AND 1980
(Each Country's Endowment as a Percent of World Total)[a]

	Year	Capital[b]	Skilled Labor[c]	Semiskilled Labor[d]	Unskilled Labor[e]	Arable Land[f]	R&D Scientists[g]
United States	1963	41.9	29.4	18.3	0.60	27.4	62.5
	1980	33.6	27.7	19.1	0.19	29.3	50.7
Canada	1963	3.8	2.5	1.7	0.06	6.5	1.6
	1980	0.0	0.0	0.1	0.00	0.1	1.0
France	1963	7.1	6.6	5.3	0.11	3.2	6.1
	1980	7.5	6.0	3.9	0.06	2.6	6.0
Germany	1963	9.1	7.1	6.8	0.14	1.3	7.5
	1980	7.7	6.9	5.5	0.08	1.1	10.0
Japan	1963	7.1	7.8	12.6	0.30	0.9	16.2
	1980	15.5	8.7	11.5	0.25	0.8	23.0
United Kingdom	1963	5.6	7.0	6.5	0.14	1.1	6.1
	1980	4.5	5.1	4.9	0.07	1.0	8.5
Total	1963	74.6	60.4	51.2	1.35	40.4	100.0
Major AICs	1980	72.7	57.3	47.0	0.68	40.9	100.0
NICs[h]	1963	6.2	19.3	24.8	86.7	37.2	N.A.
	1980	10.1	22.0	30.5	87.9	36.7	N.A.

[a]Computed from a set of 34 countries, which in 1980 accounted for over 85 percent of gross domestic product among market economies.

[b]From Harry Bowen, *Changes in the International Pattern of Factor Abundance and the Composition of Trade*, Economic Discussion Paper 8 (Department of Labor, Office of Foreign Economic Research, 1980); and updated information made available by him, based on real gross domestic investment translated into dollars at 1966 exchange rates.

[c]From Bowen, and updated information from the International Labor Organization (ILO), *Yearbook of Labor Statistics*, based on number of workers in professional and technical categories of International Standard Classification of Occupations (ISCO).

[d]From Bowen, and updated information from the ILO *Yearbook of Labor Statistics*, based on number of workers not categorized as professional-technical, but who are literate.

[e]From Bowen, and updated information from the United Nations Educational, Scientific and Cultural Organization (UNESCO), *Statistical Yearbook*, based on number of illiterate workers.

[f]From Bowen, based on measurement of land area in different climatic zones; final year reported is 1975.

[g]From data provided by the National Science Foundation; initial year is 1967 and final year is 1979. Percentages are calculated on the basis of total R&D personnel from the six countries shown, which are the principal performers of R&D among market economies.

[h]NICs are represented by Argentina, Brazil, Hong Kong, India, Korea, and Mexico in Bowen's set of countries.

opportunities for R&D scientists and engineers in Japan and some European countries. The consequence, however, is that the U.S. competitive position internationally will fall precisely in those industries in which the United States has traditionally displayed export strength.

A potentially offsetting factor is that the competitiveness of goods requiring more skilled labor (professionally and technically trained workers) should improve, since the U.S. share of skilled workers declined only slightly. So while the position

TABLE 3. RATES OF RESOURCE GROWTH, 1963–80, RELATIVE TO
TOTAL LABOR FORCE

	Capital	Skilled Labor	R&D Scientists*
United States	1.4	1.0	– 1.1
Japan	8.3	2.7	5.1
Germany	3.0	2.5	5.6
United Kingdom	3.3	1.5	5.6
France	4.9	2.7	1.9
Canada	2.0	1.3	1.1
NICs	6.2	2.6	—

*Comparison based on the period 1967–79.
Source: Calculated from data in Table 2.

of U.S. industries intensively using R&D scientists would erode somewhat, that of manufacturing and the service sectors which intensively use professional and technically trained labor should show some improvement. Semiskilled labor remains a relatively scarce resource in the United States, and the baby boom-induced increase in this resource is not likely to have a pronounced effect on U.S. competitiveness—certainly not as much as the decline in the U.S. position in R&D scientists and engineers. Goods requiring unskilled labor were not very competitive in 1963 and should have become even less so.

While trends in U.S. comparative advantage and international trade performance are more likely to be determined by changes in factor abundance among countries, as shown in Table 2, trends in industry growth rates and employment are more likely to be determined by rates of factor growth *within* a country, and these are found in Table 3. For example, while Table 2 shows a sharp drop in the U.S. global share of physical capital, Table 3 shows that the U.S. stock of physical capital grew more rapidly than the labor force. Thus, while capital-intensive industries in the United States might lose competitiveness internationally, growth rates in those industries could still be above the economywide average. In other words, changes in industrial structure should not be predicted to match exactly changes in competitiveness internationally. However, the two trends often coincide.

Turning to the other AICs, *Japan* achieved substantial progress from 1963 to 1980 in expanding its global share of R&D scientists and engineers, physical capital and skilled labor. Consequently, Japan has become more competitive in many areas of traditional U.S. strength. Further, supplies of Japanese R&D personnel, capital and skilled labor grew much more rapidly than the overall labor force, which suggests particularly fast growth for capital-intensive and high technology industries.

In *Germany* and the *United Kingdom,* the share of R&D scientists and engineers increased more rapidly than that of other resources, in sharp contrast to the United States; but this progress was not as pronounced as that of Japan. Hence, their competitive position vis à vis the United States in high technology industries should improve, but not as much as Japan's. Also, in Germany and the United Kingdom, the relative abundance of capital and skilled and semiskilled labor declined.

In *Canada* and *France,* shares of R&D personnel, capital and skilled and semiskilled labor changed less than they did in the other AICs. Therefore, Canadian and French trade performances would experience less sectoral change than those of Japan or the United States. Capital stock in France grew more rapidly but research scientists more slowly than those of other European nations. These trends suggest faster growth of traditional manufacturing activities than of high technology industries, unless government intervention alters market incentives enough to change significantly resource allocation. This qualification holds with respect to all predictions based on factor supplies alone.

Trends in the NICs

Over the past 20 years, the newly industrializing countries have become highly competitive in many labor-intensive industries. This is not surprising given their abundance of unskilled and semiskilled labor, a critical factor for competitiveness in labor-intensive manufacturing. The share of semiskilled labor in the six NICs in Table 2 rose from 25 percent in 1963 to 31 percent in 1980.

The fastest growing factors of production in the NICs during those years were physical capital and skilled labor. The rapid rates of investment they achieved over the past two decades indicate that this trend is not likely to abate. Therefore, the NICs will continue to increase their export capabilities, expanding into many of the basic heavy industries in which Japan was so successful in the 1960s and 1970s—e.g., steel and automobiles. This will force the AICs to place greater emphasis on R&D-intensive and skilled labor-intensive exports, where they will be locked in keen competition among themselves, and to turn to the application of sophisticated production technologies in basic industries.

Other Structural Considerations

The expectations based on changes in underlying structural conditions are reinforced by extending the explanation of comparative advantage given above.

One extension concerns the definition of capital abundance. When investments in new plant and equipment are the primary vehicle for implementing more advanced production processes and new ideas, international competitiveness may be dependent most on how fast capital stocks increase. Having a large capital stock may be less important than having a smaller one installed recently enough to incorporate new technological innovations. The slow growth of U.S. capital stock in recent years indicates that these considerations should reinforce changes in U.S., Japanese and NIC comparative advantages.

A more comprehensive perspective focuses on the dynamic nature of trade in many products. For instance, the United States may successfully develop a new product for its large, high income market and be in a position initially to export this good to the rest of the world. As the product becomes more standardized and production costs become a more important determinant of the competitive position of firms producing in the United States, the initial export strength may erode, and the United States may eventually become a net importer of the good. Black and white TVs are an example of this product cycle.

The resource endowment figures from Table 2 partially incorporate this concept, since the availability of R&D scientists affects the rate of product innovation and refinement in a country. However, a better understanding of the process that generates new technologies and products would allow more accurate predictions of changing competitiveness. More careful attention in this area is particularly important from a policy perspective, since government actions may favor R&D expenditures through special tax credits, but simultaneously reduce support for scientific training.

Abstracting from that distinction, as other countries have trained more scientists and engineers, they have expanded their ability to develop new products or modify and improve those developed elsewhere. In addition, as income levels in Europe and Japan have grown, the U.S. market has become less unique in terms of its large sales potential over which initial product development costs can be spread. Finally, there has been a contraction in the length of time necessary for products to become standardized enough to allow production to spread outside the United States. In other words, technology is being rapidly transferred to other countries, making the U.S. competitive advantage in any given high technology product short lived. Again, these considerations reinforce the finding that U.S. international competitiveness in high technology industries is being eroded by Japanese and European challenges.

SUMMARY

Based on these changing demand and supply considerations, then, the following trends could have been predicted in the industrial structures and international competitiveness of the United States and other AICs for the 1960s and 1970s.

- The service sectors of the AICs would expand.

- As a consequence, agriculture, mining and manufacturing as a group would be expected to decline in relative importance in these countries. But the competitiveness of these sectors individually would depend on national endowments of specific natural resources, not presented in Table 2. For example, Canadian and U.S. advantages in agriculture or Canadian and U.K. advantages in extractive activities would result in increased competitiveness and a slower decline of these sectors, relative to manufacturing, then would be expected to occur in resource-poor countries such as Japan, France or Germany.

These trends did in fact occur during the past two decades and are analyzed in Chapter 3.

Changes in international competitiveness of industries within manufacturing are not expected to be uniform. The U.S. competitive advantage in high technology activities remains substantial, but it has been weakened. Unless trends are reversed, it will continue to decline, although it will certainly not disappear. Compensating somewhat for this loss, U.S. competitiveness should improve in manufacturing and service activities requiring skilled labor. In contrast, the Japanese position will likely continue to improve in those areas. The European and Canadian situation generally lies somewhere between the Japanese and U.S. positions, and therefore the European and Canadian challenge to U.S. exports should not be expected to match that of the Japanese, at least on the basis of underlying structural conditions.

The competitiveness of the AICs as a group will continue to be challenged by the NICs in labor-intensive activities, and the NICs' challenge will continue to expand, especially in many basic heavy manufacturing activities. Some of the biggest shifts in international competitiveness will be between Japan and the United States, whereas Canada and France will likely experience smaller changes across industries in international competitive pressures.

Trends in Industry Structure and Competitiveness — an Aggregate View 3

As a starting point for the analysis of recent changes in industry structure and international competitiveness, this chapter presents a comparison of trends in production and trade for agriculture, mining, manufacturing, and the services in the United States, Japan, Germany, the United Kingdom, France, and Canada. This wide survey is useful in showing where resources are flowing as services grow and manufacturing declines in relative importance in most of the AICs.

TRENDS IN INDUSTRIAL STRUCTURE

Table 4 shows the structure of economic activity in the six AICs for four years, as available. The data are intended to illustrate longer-run trends dating back to 1960 and to cover two recent U.S. business cycles, 1969–73 and 1973–79; they are adjusted for inflation and indicate relative growth rates of the major sectors of the economies studied. These comparisons are complemented by Table 5, which shows absolute rates of growth, adjusted for inflation, in the six economies. Together the two tables give an overview of international trends in industry structure.

In 1960, the economy of the *United States* was the most service-oriented of the AICs; during the 1960s, however, that sector fell in importance and manufacturing expanded, a pattern that was reversed in the 1970s. Overall, during those two decades, the U.S. economy became more service-oriented, which is consistent with the income elasticities of demand presented in Chapter 2 and with broader-based studies of the evolution of industrial economies at more advanced stages of development.[1]

Examination of the significant components of the service sector foreshadows issues to be discussed in Part Two of this study, which focuses on government policies. Two important examples within the United States are housing and medical care. The share of national income represented by the benefits from owner-occupied housing increased over 15 percent from 1973 to 1978, which underscores the significance of public debate in the United States and abroad over the diversion of savings and investment from industrial uses to the housing sector. The rather low income elasticity of demand for housing (see Table 1, Chapter 2) implies that the growth of this industry is in no small way the consequence of monetary policies, tax breaks and financial regulations that have favored housing. Also, the income elasticity for medical services is less than one, yet growth in the demand for medical care has substantially exceeded overall income growth. Furthermore, the cost of medical services has increased more rapidly than prices in general, which ordinarily would be expected to dampen quantity demanded. One explanation of the shift

---

1 Hollis Chenery, *Structural Change and Development Policy* (New York: University Press, 1981).

TABLE 4. CHANGING PATTERNS OF PRODUCTION IN SELECTED AICs
(Shares of GDP Originating in Sector, Measured in Constant Prices*)

	Agriculture	Mining	Manufacturing	Services
United States				
1960	4.4	2.0	23.3	70.3
1969	3.2	1.7	25.5	69.7
1973	3.0	1.6	25.1	70.3
1979	2.8	1.5	24.6	71.1
Japan				
1970	6.0	0.7	29.4	63.9
1973	5.5	0.6	30.7	63.2
1979	4.2	0.5	33.1	62.2
Germany				
1960	4.9	2.4	37.0	55.7
1969	3.6	1.2	41.5	53.7
1973	3.4	1.0	40.4	55.2
1979	2.9	—	39.2	57.9
United Kingdom				
1960	2.8	3.3	28.6	65.2
1970	2.7	2.1	29.2	66.0
1973	2.7	1.7	29.0	66.6
1979	2.6	4.3	26.1	67.0
France				
1970	6.9	0.9	30.8	61.4
1973	6.4	0.7	33.5	59.4
1979	5.4	0.5	31.5	62.6
Canada				
1970	4.3	3.7	22.8	69.2
1973	3.8	3.7	23.5	69.0
1979	3.5	2.8	22.1	71.6

*Constant price measures are based on 1970 prices for France and Germany, 1971 for Canada, 1972 for the United States, and 1975 for Japan and the United Kingdom.

Sectoral definitions: agriculture includes forestry and fishing; mining includes quarrying; services include public utilities, construction, wholesale and retail trade, transport, finance, insurance and real estate, and community, social and personal services.

Sources: Calculated from data presented in the *United Nations Yearbook of National Accounts 1980*, Volume I, and from *U.S. Statistical Abstract*, various issues.

toward medical care may be that individuals who demand more care are not confronted by the full impact of higher prices, since their insurance premiums do not rise in proportion to their usage. Another may be that Medicare and Medicaid programs have increased demand by people previously unwilling or unable to pay for this care.

Manufacturing has grown fastest in *Japan,* both in absolute terms and relative to the rest of the economy. While Japan shared in the slowdown of world economic growth after 1973, its manufacturing sector continued to grow faster than its economy in general. This result contrasts with the demand-based predictions of proportionally greater service-sector growth, which is observed in all the other AICs.

However, the growth patterns of capital, labor and other resources in Japan differed from the patterns in other countries, which may offset the general prediction regarding services. In particular, the faster growth in Japan's high technology capabilities and skilled labor force may explain the greater growth in manufacturing.

Germany has undergone changes similar in many ways to those experienced by the United States. The service sector declined in importance over the 1960s, but expanded in the 1970s, while manufacturing moved in the opposite direction. Absolute rates of growth were also very similar to U.S. rates. However, both agri-

TABLE 5. ANNUAL GROWTH RATES OF REAL OUTPUT IN SELECTED AICs, 1960–79

	1960–79	1969–73	1973–79	1969–79
United States				
Gross national product	3.6	3.4	2.5	2.9
Manufacturing	3.8	3.0	2.2	2.5
Japan				
Gross domestic product	8.0	7.7	4.0	4.9
Manufacturing	—	8.8	5.6	6.3
Germany				
Gross domestic product	3.8	4.2	2.5	2.8
Manufacturing	4.2	3.6	2.0	2.3
United Kingdom				
Gross domestic product	2.6	3.4	1.6	2.2
Manufacturing	2.1	2.2	−0.5	0.6
France				
Gross domestic product	4.9	5.6	3.2	3.9
Manufacturing	—	6.4	3.1	4.2
Canada				
Gross domestic product	5.0	5.9	3.3	4.3
Manufacturing	—	5.5	2.1	3.5

Sources: *United Nations Yearbook of National Accounts 1980*, Volume II; and *U.S. Statistical Abstract*, various issues.

culture and mining declined more rapidly, allowing for the substantial increase of services in the last decade.

The *United Kingdom* is the only country in which the relative importance of the service sector expanded in each year shown. The more recent U.K. experience contrasts substantially with that of the other AICs. The share of agricultural output barely contracted, and output from the extractive sector rose phenomenally due to North Sea oil production. The decline of manufacturing was accelerated by a negative absolute growth rate since 1973. Thus, even though Germany and the United Kingdom had rather similar changes in various types of capital and labor endowments, the explanation of their changing economic structure requires additional information on natural resource deposits.

TABLE 6. CHANGING STRUCTURE OF INTERNATIONAL TRADE, 1973 AND 1979
          ($ U.S. Bill.)

	Year	Exports	Percent of Total	Imports	Percent of Total	Exports/ GDP from Sector	Imports/ Apparent Consumption	Exports/ Imports
United States	1973							
Total		$70.5	100.0	$69.5	100.0	0.05	0.05	1.01
Primary		23.9	33.9	22.7	32.7	0.33	0.31	1.05
Manufactures		46.6	66.1	46.8	67.3	0.14	0.14	1.00
Fuel		—	—	8.0	11.6	—	—	—
	1979							
Total		$173.6	100.0	$217.5	100.0	0.07	0.09	0.80
Primary		52.7	30.4	95.2	43.8	0.37	0.51	0.55
Manufactures		120.9	69.6	122.3	56.2	0.21	0.21	0.99
Fuel		—	—	63.4	29.1	—	—	—
Japan	1973							
Total		$36.7	100.0	$38.1	100.0	0.09	0.09	0.96
Primary		0.8	2.2	26.4	69.3	0.03	0.50	0.03
Manufactures		35.9	97.8	11.7	30.7	0.20	0.07	3.08
Fuel		—	—	8.3	21.7	—	—	—
	1979							
Total		$103.0	100.0	$110.1	100.0	0.10	0.11	0.94
Primary		2.9	2.8	82.6	75.0	0.06	0.63	0.04
Manufactures		100.0	97.2	27.5	25.0	0.34	0.12	3.64
Fuel		—	—	45.4	41.0	—	—	—
Germany	1973							
Total		$67.4	100.0	$54.5	100.0	0.20	0.16	1.24
Primary		6.3	9.3	21.7	39.8	0.44	0.73	0.29
Manufactures		61.1	90.7	32.8	60.2	0.46	0.31	1.86
Fuel		—	—	5.9	10.9	—	—	—
	1979							
Total		$171.4	100.0	$157.7	100.0	0.23	0.21	1.09
Primary		18.0	10.5	62.9	39.9	—	—	0.29
Manufactures		153.4	89.5	94.8	60.1	0.54	0.42	1.62
Fuel		—	—	30.8	19.5	—	—	—

Continued, p. 16

During the 1970s, *France* enjoyed more rapid growth than most European countries, but its economic structure changed less than the others. Both services and manufacturing expanded slightly, at the expense of agriculture and mining. This pattern of fairly balanced growth coincides with predictions of little change in international competitiveness across sectors.

Canada now appears to be the most service-oriented of the economies studied, owing to rapid growth of the service sector since 1973. During the 1970s, manufacturing declined in relative importance, as did agriculture and mining in spite of strong Canadian comparative advantages in those sectors.

In summary, the evolution of these six economies has been consistent with the general demand thesis in favor of services. The effect of changing factor supplies is more difficult to relate to these results, because large differences in input requirements, aside from natural resources, have not been well established at such broad levels of aggregation. Relationships between changes in economic structure

TABLE 6 continued. Changing Structure of International Trade

	Year	Exports	Percent of Total	Imports	Percent of Total	Exports/ GDP from Sector	Imports/ Apparent Consumption	Exports/ Imports
United Kingdom	1973							
Total		$30.5	100.0	$38.9	100.0	0.17	0.21	0.79
Primary		4.1	13.4	16.7	42.9	0.59	0.86	0.25
Manufactures		26.4	86.6	22.2	57.1	0.57	0.53	1.19
Fuel		—	—	1.7	10.8	—	—	—
	1979							
Total		$90.5	100.0	$102.5	100.0	0.23	0.25	0.88
Primary		28.1	20.0	34.5	33.7	1.14	1.11	0.81
Manufactures		72.4	80.0	65.0	66.3	0.75	0.74	1.07
Fuel		—	—	12.2	11.8	—	—	—
France	1973							
Total		$35.4	100.0	$36.8	100.0	0.14	0.15	0.96
Primary		9.3	26.3	13.0	35.3	0.50	0.58	0.72
Manufactures		26.1	73.7	23.8	64.7	0.37	0.35	1.10
Fuel		—	—	4.6	12.3	—	—	—
	1979							
Total		$98.0	100.0	$106.7	100.0	0.17	0.18	0.92
Primary		21.9	22.3	42.3	39.6	0.71	0.82	0.52
Manufactures		76.1	77.7	64.4	60.4	0.49	0.45	1.18
Fuel		—	—	23.0	21.3	—	—	—
Canada	1973							
Total		$25.2	100.0	$23.3	100.0	0.20	0.19	1.08
Primary		11.4	45.2	4.4	18.9	1.11	1.33	2.59
Manufactures		13.8	54.8	18.9	81.1	0.55	0.63	0.73
Fuel		—	—	1.3	5.6	—	—	—
	1979							
Total		$56.1	100.0	$52.6	100.0	0.24	0.23	1.07
Primary		24.7	44.0	11.2	21.3	1.24	1.75	2.21
Manufactures		31.4	56.0	41.4	78.7	0.71	0.76	0.76
Fuel		—	—	4.9	9.2	—	—	—

Sources: *OECD Trade by Commodities*, various issues; and *United Nations Yearbook of National Accounts*, various issues.

and the availability of capital and various types of labor can more readily be determined within the manufacturing sector, where industry input requirements can be assessed more precisely and clearer differences across industries can be demonstrated.

TRENDS IN INTERNATIONAL COMPETITIVENESS

As in the case of industrial structure, examination of shifts in international competitiveness at a broad level can provide a useful perspective from which to assess changes in particular industries.

For 1973 and 1979, Table 6 shows the relative dependence of the six economies upon foreign trade and the changing competitiveness of broad sectors of each country. The countries least dependent on trade are the United States and Japan.

Contrary to the common complaint that few products are developed for the Japanese home market and that the country is dependent on high export growth to improve its economic position, Japan's export dependence (even within manufacturing) is in fact smaller than that of the European countries or Canada. For all countries, the decade of the 1970s continued to be characterized by trade expanding at a faster rate than national output.

Over an horizon of 10 years or less, changes in the international competitiveness of the AICs' aggregate manufacturing sectors are difficult to explain solely on the basis of shifts in physical capital, labor force characteristics and the availability of R&D scientists and engineers. Other changes occur, affecting international prices and exchange rates in particular, that may override shifts in underlying structural conditions:

- changes in service account payments or large international movements of financial assets, which may result from international differences in macroeconomic policies and interests rates or political stability;

- adjustments to large changes in prices of oil, other natural resources and agricultural goods, which may alter the importance of trade in nonmanufactured goods.

A fall in the value of the U.S. dollar internationally can improve the competitiveness of U.S. goods, if this depreciation is not offset by greater inflation in the prices of those goods. At an aggregate level, economists generally expect the two effects to cancel in the longer run, so that an exchange-rate depreciation will not give a permanent advantage to a country's exporters and producers of import-competing goods. Particular sectors within an economy will be affected differently if all prices do not rise proportionally, however.

The value of the dollar is determined by the international flows of services and capital in addition to goods. For example, when the United States has a balanced current account, the merchandise trade balance is often substantially negative and offset by net exports of services. Services include the income from U.S. foreign investment and because that income has grown over time, the U.S. ability to run trade deficits without the dollar depreciating has increased; specifically, income earned on foreign investments increased from 22 percent of merchandise exports in 1965 to 34 percent in 1980.

In addition, the demand and supply of dollars attributable to trade in goods and services may be dominated by international capital flows due to international asset movements. The United States can run a deficit on trade in goods and services if foreigners want to buy U.S. assets and lend to U.S. individuals and companies. If U.S. monetary policy results in higher interest rates on U.S. financial instruments, the U.S. dollar will appreciate, or imports of goods and services will rise. Either result causes a decline in the competitive position of U.S. producers of traded goods and services, primarily manufacturers. This factor has been relevant in explaining the U.S. experience since 1979, as rising real interest rates in the United States have contributed to a substantial appreciation of the U.S. dollar and a corresponding decline in the competitiveness of U.S. producers of all traded goods.

Changes in the competitive positions of the manufacturing sectors of the AICs have not been uniform. One measure of this phenomenon are the ratios of manufactured exports to imports:

Ratio of Manufactured Exports to Imports			
	1969	1973	1979
United States	1.15	1.00	0.99
Japan	3.40	3.08	3.64
Germany	1.80	1.86	1.62
United Kingdom	1.52	1.19	1.07
France	1.02	1.10	1.18
Canada	0.79	0.73	0.76

From 1969 to 1979, the competitive performance of overall manufacturing in Japan and France improved, while it deteriorated in the United States, Germany and the United Kingdom, and remained fairly constant in Canada. These mixed results are not surprising, since the AICs still account for the majority of trade in manufactures, and one country's gain in competitiveness is offset by another's loss. Of course, the manufacturing exports of all AICs could grow more rapidly than imports if, for example, exports to oil-producing countries were to account for a large enough share of trade. Apparently, this was not the case, and the AICs cannot be regarded as a single block in assessing the competitive pressures they have faced.

The decrease in manufacturing competitiveness in the *United States,* even over a period when the value of the U.S. dollar declined, reflects the changing comparative advantage of U.S. agriculture and services relative to manufactured goods, as well as the increasing importance of investment income and capital flows for the United States. The latter imply a higher value of the dollar and a less competitive position of manufacturing than otherwise might have been expected on the basis of cost considerations.

The skewed nature of *Japanese* trade in manufacturing conforms to the allegation of many in the U.S. private sector that it is difficult to export to Japan. The overall Japanese trade balance declined only slightly over this period, showing that a higher oil import bill essentially was paid for by greater manufactured exports.

Another allegation often leveled at the Japanese is that the yen has been undervalued in order to make Japanese goods more competitive internationally. That policy probably would promote tradeable manufactured goods relative to other goods in the economy, although trade in services such as transportation, communication and banking cannot be ignored. Bank of Japan sales of yen, and consequent increases in foreign exchange holdings, are one explicit measure of Japanese efforts to depress the price of the yen. Japanese official reserves did not grow continually over the period, as would be the case if the goal of an undervalued yen had been pursued single-mindedly. Instead, reserve losses occurred in 1973, 1975 and 1979, which reflect attempts to support the value of the yen. From 1979 to 1982, official reserves grew, and Western dissatisfaction with Japanese policy increased correspondingly. In addition to this readily quantifiable indication of Japanese policy, a more complete analysis would require attention to other government practices as well.

In *Germany* and the *United Kingdom,* manufacturing competitiveness declined from 1969 to 1979. The emergence of the United Kingdom as a net exporter of oil after 1973 helps explain manufacturing's deteriorating performance. In both countries, shares of world capital and skilled labor also declined.

Conversely, *French* manufacturing competitiveness increased over the period, as did its share of world capital stock. That factor apparently is of particular significance in terms of ability to adopt new technologies in manufacturing industries. Finally, competitiveness of the *Canadian* manufacturing sector remained fairly constant, in spite of the predicted potential expansion of its many primary producers. The lack of any big shift in Canadian competitiveness is consistent with the relatively constant shares of inputs shown in Table 2, Chapter 2.

In summary, changing competitiveness internationally in the short run can be significantly influenced by macroeconomic policies and conditions, such as exchange-rate variations, which are independent of the relative availability of capital and other factors of production across countries. Nevertheless, if appropriate measures of mineral reserves and other natural resources had been included in the data reported in Chapter 2, the factor supply framework presented there would have predicted the changing competitiveness of manufacturing in most countries. In any event, generalizations at this level provide a useful perspective for the focus of the next chapter on the experience of particular industries; growth and competitiveness of a single industry should be assessed not only in absolute terms but also relative to the average performance of all manufacturing.

Trends within Manufacturing 4

The divergent performance of the AICs' manufacturing sectors examined in Chapter 3 allows a general evaluation of changes in international competitiveness. But changes in the relative importance and trade performance of particular industries within manufacturing better illustrate the kinds of structural changes and adjustment problems faced by the industrialized countries.

As import competition and sluggish demand cause some industries to grow more slowly than others, or even contract, labor and capital do not move easily to new uses; certainly they often bear significant costs, as does society as a whole. Studies of workers displaced by imports show that in some U.S. industries, such as footwear, a significant number of workers are unable to move geographically and possess few skills demanded by other industries; when those workers lose their jobs, they simply drop out of the labor force. Of course, the slower a trade-impacted industry grows, the greater such hardships will be, especially in periods of generally high unemployment. This situation has plagued European countries in particular since the early 1970s, as democratic governments have come under substantial pressure to slow down the rate of change in the economy (e.g., slow down the decline of trade-impacted industries). Over the last several years, these hardships have also become all too common in the U.S. Midwest and Northeast.

This chapter discusses changes in the industrial structure and international competitive positions of industries within the manufacturing sector over the period 1969–79. Specifically, the performance of 20 industries within the manufacturing sectors of the United States, Japan, Germany, the United Kingdom, and Canada are analyzed, while for France the limited data available allow only more aggregate summary comparisons to be made. The separate industries listed by International Standard Industrial Classification Codes are:

transport equipment (384)
electrical machinery (383)
professional goods (385)
machinery, not elsewhere classified, nec. (382)
industrial chemicals (351)
other chemicals (352)
rubber products (355)
plastic products (356)
petroleum refining and coal products (353–354)
nonferrous metals (372)
metal products (381)
pottery, glass and other nonmetallic products (361–369)
wood products (331)
iron and steel (371)
food and beverages (311–313)

paper products (341)
textiles (321)
apparel (322)
leather products (323)
footwear (324).

The questions raised at the outset of the study will be examined in this chapter.
- To what extent do all developed countries face a similar set of competitive pressures?

- How have U.S. competitive advantages and disadvantages changed?

- How are changes in U.S. competitiveness in manufacturing related to changes in industry structure in the United States and elsewhere? In particular, have other AICs expanded their capabilities more rapidly in areas where the United States has traditionally enjoyed strength? Have other AICs' industrial structures become more similar to that of the United States, making more difficult the maintenance of U.S. competitive advantages in areas of traditional strength?

- To what extent have other countries better responded to competitive pressures by altering their industry structures more rapidly than the United States?

Chapter 2 demonstrated that, in one sense, the economies of the United States and the other AICs are evolving in a similar pattern due to the common demand factors favoring the service sector. However, differences in the availability of land and natural resources among these countries have resulted in differences in the growth and international competitiveness of agriculture, mining and manufacturing. Furthermore, as a result of the trends in the supply of capital, R&D personnel and other types of labor, the U.S. experience within the manufacturing sector has not paralleled that of the other AICs. Growth in the United States has been slower in precisely the resources required most by industries in which the United States has traditionally displayed a strong competitive position.

To predict the way industry structure and competitiveness are changing in response to changes in structural conditions and to assess how well these predictions are fulfilled, the 20 manufacturing industries were divided into 3 groups. The groupings were based on the individual industries' use of R&D personnel, physical capital and various types of labor (to be discussed more fully):
- *technology-intensive industries* undertaking relatively large amounts of R&D and using relatively more skilled labor;

- *standardized goods industries* producing products with large amounts of capital, and generally undertaking less R&D than the first group but using more capital;

- *labor-intensive industries* using larger amounts of less skilled labor, generally undertaking less R&D and using less skilled labor and capital than the first two groups.

Changes in patterns of international competitiveness and industry structure in the five countries studied turned out to be remarkably consistent with patterns projected on the basis of changes in the relative availability (global shares) of R&D scientists and engineers, physical capital and various types of labor. But some exceptions prevailed that may be explained by government intervention, and some expected changes seemed more pronounced than anticipated, which may also be explained by government incentives.

From 1969 to 1979, the strong U.S. export position in technology-intensive goods declined, while Japan's progress in this area was unsurpassed. As previously explained, German and U.K. competitiveness internationally were expected to improve vis à vis the United States, but not by as much as for Japan. In fact, however, the Japanese gain was so strong that the German and U.K. competitive positions declined too. In spite of the below average growth of R&D personnel in France, French competitiveness strengthened over the decade, although at a slower rate than the Japanese and largely as a result of the stronger competitive position of manufacturing as a whole. Canadian international competitiveness did not change much in this area.

The United States experienced its greatest competitive decline in the standardized goods sector, as expected given its declining share of global capital. Japan's competitiveness in this sector also eroded significantly, a surprising result considering its rapid rate of capital accumulation in recent years. However, the Japanese government intentionally adopted policies to steer capital and other resources away from its capital-intensive standardized goods industries. The German and U.K. performances improved somewhat, but by the end of the 1970s those countries still exported less standardized goods than they imported. French competitiveness also increased, and even more rapidly in this area than in technology-intensive goods. The Japanese and U.S. experience reflects not simply reduced competitiveness relative to the other AICs, but also the pressure of greater exports of NIC capital-intensive standardized goods-producing industries in the 1970s, as well as, in Japan's case, the government's policies just noted.

Finally, in labor-intensive industries, the United States, Germany, the United Kingdom, and Canada continued to import substantially more than they exported. Moreover, Japan, within the short period of a decade, changed from a significant net exporter to a virtually balanced trade position in labor-intensive goods, and France became a net importer.

INDUSTRY CHARACTERISTICS

The 20 industries to be analyzed include practically all manufacturing activities, although differences in reporting procedures across countries caused the omission of a few industry categories (e.g., tobacco, furniture and fixtures, printing and publishing, and miscellaneous manufacturing). These 20 industries are not expected to experience the same changes in competitiveness or grow at the same rate, being affected differently by changes in underlying structural conditions depending on the nature of demand for their products and the importance of various production inputs. Differences in input requirements are more pronounced than differences in demand elasticities discussed earlier; thus, input requirements are used to group industries to evaluate changing patterns of international competitiveness and industrial structure.

TABLE 7. U.S. INDUSTRY INPUT CHARACTERISTICS, 1979

Industry	1 R&D Expenditure/ Value Added	2 Employment/ Value Added	3 Payroll/ Value Added	4 Human Capital/ Value Added
Transport equipment (384)	13.2	.024	.48	.34
Electrical machinery (383)	11.0	.029	.44	.27
Professional goods (385)	9.4	.024	.40	.24
Machinery, nec. (382)	9.0	.026	.44	.29
Industrial chemicals (351)	8.6	.014	.27	.19
Other chemicals (352)	6.1	.012	.22	.15
Average, technology-intensive goods	10.1	.023	.40	.27
Rubber products (355)	4.9	.030	.48	.30
Plastic products (356)	4.8	.034	.41	.22
Petroleum refining and coal products (353–354)	3.8	.005	.12	.09
Nonferrous metals (372)	3.5	.022	.39	.26
Metal products (381)	2.4	.029	.45	.28
Pottery, glass, etc. (361–369)	2.3	.027	.40	.25
Wood products (331)	2.0	.037	.45	.24
Iron and steel (371)	1.6	.024	.52	.38
Food and beverages (311–313)	1.4	.023	.32	.18
Paper products (341)	1.4	.024	.40	.26
Average, standardized goods	3.2	.025	.38	.24
Textiles (321)	1.0	.046	.49	.22
Apparel (322)	.8	.060	.49	.14
Leather products (323)	N.A.	.056	.49	.16
Footwear (324)	N.A.	.060	.49	.15
Average, labor-intensive goods	N.A.	.054	.49	.17

nec. = not elsewhere classified.
Source: U.S. Department of Commerce, *1980 Annual Survey of Manufactures*.

U.S. industry data for 1979 show how input requirements differ across industries (see Table 7). The 20 industries are listed by their R&D intensity (reported in the first column) as measured by R&D expenditure divided by industry value added. This variable is by no means the only important characteristic to consider in evaluating an industry's prospects. However, it allows a grouping of industries into three separate categories which require other inputs in substantially different proportions that are also important in evaluating changes in trade and production over time. Measures of the different input requirements are explained next; then differences among the three broad industry groupings are discussed more completely.

The second column in Table 7 reports employment divided by value added, which indicates the labor intensity of production—e.g., a higher number shows relatively greater importance for labor in the production process. By this measure, apparel and footwear are the most labor-intensive U.S. industries. Chapter 2 distinguished among different types of labor according to skill levels, and columns three and four do so along similar lines. Payroll divided by value added shows the importance not only of the number of workers employed but also of the wage rate paid. This ratio can be used to estimate the return to labor due to extra productivity beyond what an unskilled worker would earn. When additional education or on-the-job training allows a substantial increase in the worker's productivity, and a corresponding increase in the amount an employer is willing to pay for this service, that extra payment is referred to as a return to human capital; those estimates are reported in column four.

The payroll to value-added ratio also demonstrates the importance of capital in production, since the remaining value added represents a return to capital or property owners. A low payroll to value-added ratio, such as the entry observed for petroleum refining and coal products, implies a relatively capital-intensive industry. This interpretation is approximate, though, because it assumes that returns to capital equalize across industries so that a smaller share of value added attributable to capital implies a smaller amount of capital used in the industry. That situation may not hold in the short run when capital is immobile in an industry and must accept a lower rate of return (which may be relevant in interpreting the low capital intensity indicated for the steel industry).

Furthermore, the return to property may represent a return to proprietary information, as opposed to a physical asset. A low payroll to value-added ratio need not indicate an industry requiring large amounts of physical capital, then, if returns to the development of new technology are important. The R&D variable shown in column one suggests the importance of developing new processes and new products within the industry; alternatively, it might be interpreted as an indicator of technology-intensive industries.

The three major industry groups were formed as follows. Industries with ratios of research and development to value added exceeding 6 percent were designated as technology intensive. Industries with values of 1 percent or less were listed as labor intensive, due to the larger amounts of labor used. The remaining industries were classified as standardized goods, since this sector includes products such as wood, paper, steel, glass, and gasoline.

The data in Table 7 indicate that industries in the technology-intensive sector usually undertook more R&D activity and generally used more skilled labor than other industries. The standardized goods group had the lowest entry for payroll/value added or, correspondingly, the greatest return to property income. Since the R&D intensity of that sector was not particularly great, it can be considered the most capital intensive of the three groups. The labor-intensive sector required the smallest amount of human capital and was not particularly capital-intensive or research-oriented. Therefore, any prediction of the changing competitive position of the research-intensive group will be most dependent on the relative availability of both R&D personnel and skilled labor generally. Competitiveness of standardized goods will be particularly related to the availability of physical capital, while the position of labor-intensive goods will be most closely tied to the availability of semiskilled labor.

COMPARISONS OF CHANGING INTERNATIONAL COMPETITIVENESS AND INDUSTRY STRUCTURE

For 1969, 1973 and 1979, Table 8 reports export-import ratios for the 20 individual industries and 3 major industry groups for the United States, Japan, Germany, the United Kingdom, and Canada. For the same years and countries, Table 9 reports shares of manufacturing output for the 20 industries.

TABLE 8. CHANGES IN INTERNATIONAL COMPETITIVENESS, EXPORT-IMPORT RATIOS

Industry	United States 1969	1973	1979
Transport equipment (384)	1.17	.90	.93
Electrical machinery (383)	1.57	1.60	1.17
Professional goods (385)	N.A.	N.A.	3.27
Machinery, nec. (382)	2.77	2.24	2.22
Industrial chemicals (351)	2.70	2.24	2.12
Other chemicals (352)	2.82	2.50	2.73
Average, technology-intensive goods	1.78	1.48	1.52
Rubber products (355)	1.25	.54	.49
Plastic products (356)	5.95	4.94	5.19
Petroleum refining and coal products (353–354)	3.73	.17	.09
Nonferrous metals (372)	.56	.43	.35
Metal products (381)	1.01	.78	.83
Pottery, glass, etc. (361–369)	.44	.46	.46
Wood products (331)	.29	.38	.30
Iron and steel (371)	.54	.43	.29
Food and beverages (311–313)	.28	.27	.33
Paper products (341)	.54	.63	.56
Average, standardized goods	.53	.41	.39
Textiles (321)	.56	.78	1.39
Apparel (322)	.20	.13	.15
Leather products (323)	.63	.69	.89
Footwear (324)	.02	.02	.03
Average, labor-intensive goods	.33	.33	.38
Average, all manufacturing trade*	1.15	1.00	.99
Average, all merchandise trade	1.05	1.01	.80

*Industries not shown separately are tobacco products, furniture and fixtures, printing and publishing, and other miscellaneous products.
Source: OECD, *Trade by Commodities, Series C*, various years.

TABLE 8 continued. Export-Import Ratios

Industry	Japan 1969	1973	1979
Transport equipment (384)	12.50	21.70	15.10
Electrical machinery (383)	9.18	8.38	12.40
Professional goods (385)	N.A.	N.A.	1.65
Machinery, nec. (382)	1.77	2.71	5.89
Industrial chemicals (351)	2.40	3.92	1.69
Other chemicals (352)	.49	.44	.68
Average, technology-intensive goods	3.41	4.58	5.67
Rubber products (355)	21.40	9.78	7.45
Plastic products (356)	5.66	2.76	3.43
Petroleum refining and coal products (353–354)	.12	.10	.02
Nonferrous metals (372)	.20	.19	.32
Metal products (381)	11.47	7.85	6.75
Pottery, glass, etc. (361–369)	2.92	.97	1.34
Wood products (331)	1.98	.25	.61
Iron and steel (371)	9.29	22.80	15.70
Food and beverages (311–313)	.32	.20	.10
Paper products (341)	3.38	2.23	2.12
Average, standardized goods	1.50	1.22	1.09
Textiles (321)	10.30	2.16	1.90
Apparel (322)	11.10	.64	.19
Leather products (323)	2.00	1.13	.97
Footwear (324)	26.80	.78	.15
Average, labor-intensive goods	14.92	1.60	1.04
Average, all manufacturing trade*	3.40	3.08	3.64
Average, all merchandise trade	1.06	.96	.94

TABLE 8 continued. Export-Import Ratios

Industry	Germany 1969	1973	1979
Transport equipment (384)	3.69	3.64	2.82
Electrical machinery (383)	2.41	2.26	1.89
Professional goods (385)	N.A.	N.A.	1.93
Machinery, nec. (382)	3.57	3.77	3.09
Industrial chemicals (351)	1.87	1.88	1.59
Other chemicals (352)	3.14	2.89	2.32
Average, technology-intensive goods	3.04	3.02	2.41
Rubber products (355)	1.24	1.46	1.22
Plastic products (356)	2.20	2.10	1.78
Petroleum refining and coal products (353–354)	.46	.27	.18
Nonferrous metals (372)	.39	.60	.78
Metal products (381)	3.13	2.29	2.09
Pottery, glass, etc. (361–369)	1.34	1.09	1.15
Wood products (331)	.78	.57	.62
Iron and steel (371)	1.50	1.77	1.69
Food and beverages (311–313)	.18	.25	.41
Paper products (341)	.51	.71	.78
Average, standardized goods	.71	.82	.84
Textiles (321)	.97	1.10	.94
Apparel (322)	.47	.36	.35
Leather products (323)	.63	.73	.75
Footwear (324)	.38	.25	.20
Average, labor-intensive goods	.73	.70	.59
Average, all manufacturing trade*	1.80	1.86	1.62
Average, all merchandise trade	1.17	1.24	1.09

TABLE 8 continued. Export-Import Ratios

Industry	United Kingdom 1969	1973	1979
Transport equipment (384)	3.08	1.16	1.10
Electrical machinery (383)	2.13	1.08	1.17
Professional goods (385)	N.A.	N.A.	1.24
Machinery, nec. (382)	2.63	1.87	1.75
Industrial chemicals (351)	1.00	.68	1.17
Other chemicals (352)	2.37	2.74	2.00
Average, technology-intensive goods	3.16	1.41	1.39
Rubber products (355)	2.94	2.12	1.41
Plastic products (356)	1.39	1.10	.94
Petroleum refining and coal products (353–354)	.65	.92	.91
Nonferrous metals (372)	.51	.82	.73
Metal products (381)	2.83	1.65	1.54
Pottery, glass, etc. (361–369)	1.17	1.18	1.11
Wood products (331)	.08	.06	.16
Iron and steel (371)	1.64	1.16	1.05
Food and beverages (311–313)	.23	.30	.44
Paper products (341)	.39	.32	.35
Average, standardized goods	.60	.67	.76
Textiles (321)	1.45	1.14	.79
Apparel (322)	.86	.54	.63
Leather products (323)	1.22	1.23	1.14
Footwear (324)	.94	.42	.32
Average, labor-intensive goods	1.22	.89	.71
Average, all manufacturing trade*	1.52	1.19	1.07
Average, all merchandise trade	.88	.79	.88

TABLE 8 continued. Export-Import Ratios

Industry	Canada 1969	1973	1979
Transport equipment (384)	1.09	1.04	1.01
Electrical machinery (383)	.51	.44	.49
Professional goods (385)	N.A.	N.A.	.37
Machinery, nec. (382)	.49	.50	.53
Industrial chemicals (351)	.54	.52	1.03
Other chemicals (352)	.79	.73	.83
Average, technology-intensive goods	.78	.74	.77
Rubber products (355)	.18	.30	.59
Plastic products (356)	.16	.17	.31
Petroleum refining and coal products (353–354)	.15	1.24	4.97
Nonferrous metals (372)	4.61	4.45	3.93
Metal products (381)	.34	.42	.58
Pottery, glass, etc. (361–369)	.20	.36	.49
Wood products (331)	1.99	1.60	2.74
Iron and steel (371)	.64	.74	.93
Food and beverages (311–313)	.72	.84	.78
Paper products (341)	11.30	7.39	7.80
Average, standardized goods	1.29	1.29	1.38
Textiles (321)	.16	.19	.18
Apparel (322)	.38	.37	.23
Leather products (323)	.35	.32	.27
Footwear (324)	.16	.19	.15
Average, labor-intensive goods	.22	.24	.20
Average, all manufacturing trade*	.79	.73	.76
Average, all merchandise trade	1.05	1.08	1.07

TABLE 9. CHANGES IN INDUSTRIAL STRUCTURE, INDUSTRY SHARES OF TOTAL
MANUFACTURING VALUE ADDED

Industry	United States 1969	1973	1979
Transport equipment (384)	.134	.125	.121
Electrical machinery (383)	.082	.089	.092
Professional goods (385)	.030	.030	.033
Machinery, nec. (382)	.110	.115	.119
Industrial chemicals (351)	.040	.047	.053
Other chemicals (352)	.044	.046	.053
Average, technology-intensive goods	.439	.451	.471
Rubber products (355)	.015	.016	.015
Plastic products (356)	.013	.018	.026
Petroleum refining and coal products (353–354)	.019	.019	.018
Nonferrous metals (372)	.019	.018	.016
Metal products (381)	.069	.068	.068
Pottery, glass, etc. (361–369)	.033	.033	.034
Wood products (331)	.024	.023	.021
Iron and steel (371)	.053	.049	.038
Food and beverages (311–313)	.101	.097	.103
Paper products (341)	.038	.038	.035
Total, standardized goods	.383	.378	.374
Textiles (321)	.035	.039	.033
Apparel (322)	.033	.030	.029
Leather products (323)	.003	.002	.002
Footwear (324)	.007	.005	.003
Total, labor-intensive goods	.077	.076	.067
Index of average level of output, all manufacturing*	84.8	100.0	117.9

*Industries not shown separately are tobacco products, furniture and fixtures, printing and publishing, and other miscellaneous products.
Source: *United Nations, Yearbook of Industrial Statistics*, Volume I, various issues.

TABLE 9 continued. Industry Shares of Manufacturing Value Added

Industry	1969	Japan 1973	1979
Transport equipment (384)	.088	.097	.099
Electrical machinery (383)	.096	.106	.133
Professional goods (385)	.013	.014	.032
Machinery, nec. (382)	.113	.112	.120
Industrial chemicals (351)	.051	.052	.055
Other chemicals (352)	.035	.040	.053
Total, technology-intensive goods	.396	.420	.402
Rubber products (355)	.013	.012	.014
Plastic products (356)	.022	.026	.027
Petroleum refining and coal products (353–354)	.014	.015	.014
Nonferrous metals (372)	.023	.023	.024
Metal products (381)	.064	.069	.068
Pottery, glass, etc. (361–369)	.049	.051	.050
Wood products (331)	.050	.036	.031
Iron and steel (371)	.082	.081	.080
Food and beverages (311–313)	.102	.081	.085
Paper products (341)	.031	.029	.031
Total, standardized goods	.449	.424	.423
Textiles (321)	.082	.068	.060
Apparel (322)	.018	.015	.014
Leather products (323)	.003	.003	.003
Footwear (324)	.002	.002	.002
Total, labor-intensive goods	.106	.088	.078
Index of average level of output, all manufacturing*	68.4	100.0	113.7

TABLE 9 continued. Industry Shares of Manufacturing Value Added

Industry	1969	Germany 1973	1979
Transport equipment (384)	.092	.094	.104
Electrical machinery (383)	.090	.104	.107
Professional goods (385)	.021	.019	.018
Machinery, nec. (382)	.134	.123	.118
Industrial chemicals (351)	.076	.086	.091
Other chemicals (352)			
Total, technology-intensive goods	.413	.425	.437
Rubber products (355)	.013	.012	.012
Plastic products (356)	.015	.020	.026
Petroleum refining and coal products (353–354)	.055	.056	.055
Nonferrous metals (372)	.007	.006	.007
Metal products (381)	.058	.056	.052
Pottery, glass, etc. (361–369)	.052	.053	.051
Wood products (331)	.043	.042	.042
Iron and steel (371)	.085	.078	.068
Food and beverages (311–313)	.100	.099	.101
Paper products (341)	.021	.021	.022
Total, standardized goods	.448	.445	.434
Textiles (321)	.037	.034	.031
Apparel (322)	.028	.024	.019
Leather products (323)	.015	.010	.009
Footwear (324)	.015	.010	.007
Total, labor-intensive goods	.095	.077	.066
Index of average level of output, all manufacturing*	84.8	100.0	109.2

TABLE 9 continued. Industry Shares of Manufacturing Value Added

Industry	United Kingdom		
	1969	1973	1979
Transport equipment (384)	.122	.111	.098
Electrical machinery (383)	.074	.082	.083
Professional goods (385)	.016	.017	.021
Machinery, nec. (382)	.097	.092	.098
Industrial chemicals (351)	.054	.062	.067
Other chemicals (352)	.030	.036	.046
Total, technology-intensive goods	.392	.399	.413
Rubber products (355)	.017	.016	.017
Plastic products (356)	.011	.014	.018
Petroleum refining and coal products (353–354)	.015	.016	.015
Nonferrous metals (372)	.020	.020	.019
Metal products (381)	.079	.070	.065
Pottery, glass, etc. (361–369)	.041	.045	.041
Wood products (331)	.017	.020	.017
Iron and steel (371)	.062	.055	.046
Food and beverages (311–313)	.119	.119	.130
Paper products (341)	.032	.031	.029
Total, standardized goods	.411	.405	.396
Textiles (321)	.058	.055	.046
Apparel (322)	.021	.023	.026
Leather products (323)	.005	.004	.004
Footwear (324)	.008	.008	.007
Total, labor-intensive goods	.092	.089	.083
Index of average level of output, all manufacturing*	90.7	100.0	96.3

TABLE 9 continued. Industry Shares of Manufacturing Value Added

Industry	Canada		
	1969	1973	1979
Transport equipment (384)	.109	.119	.112
Electrical machinery (383)	.070	.069	.063
Professional goods (385)	.010	.011	.012
Machinery, nec. (382)	.049	.048	.060
Industrial chemicals (351)	.025	.025	.028
Other chemicals (352)	.037	.039	.043
Total, technology-intensive goods	.300	.311	.318
Rubber products (355)	.017	.016	.017
Plastic products (356)	.010	.012	.013
Petroleum refining and coal products (353–354)	.017	.020	.019
Nonferrous metals (372)	.033	.028	.024
Metal products (381)	.076	.074	.073
Pottery, glass, etc. (361–369)	.028	.037	.026
Wood products (331)	.059	.064	.068
Iron and steel (371)	.047	.047	.048
Food and beverages (311–313)	.148	.137	.135
Paper products (341)	.084	.079	.080
Total, standardized goods	.519	.514	.503
Textiles (321)	.042	.043	.042
Apparel (322)	.030	.030	.029
Leather products (323)	.003	.003	.004
Footwear (324)	.005	.005	.004
Total, labor-intensive goods	.080	.081	.077
Index of average level of output, all manufacturing*	81.4	100.0	113.6

Analyzing this amount of data can be tedious. One useful approach is to focus first on the major group averages, which Table 10 presents. When anomalous results are found, however, attention must turn to the individual industry data that show the many diverse activities and products making up the three groups. For example, the transport equipment industry includes passenger automobiles, shipbuilding and aircraft; the latter is very research-intensive while the other two are somewhat less so. Thus, the technology-intensive industries also contain some capital-intensive standardized goods. Nevertheless, differences in input characteristics are substantial across the three major groups, and the consequent differences in their international trade and growth performance are important.

Changes in the AICs as a Group

During the 1970s, the AICs continued to lose ground to the NICs in a widening range of labor-intensive activities. In the industries of traditional opportunity and greatest interest to emerging Third World countries—textiles, apparel, footwear, and various other leather products—the AICs as a group continued to increase their absorption of imports more rapidly than their exports grew, and to reduce the share of manufacturing activity devoted to those products (see Table 10). Only

TABLE 10. SUMMARY OF CHANGES IN INTERNATIONAL COMPETITIVENESS AND INDUSTRY STRUCTURE

A. Changes in International Competitiveness: Export-Import Ratios

		U.S.	Japan	Germany	U.K.	France	Canada
Technology-intensive	1969	1.78	3.41	3.04	3.16	1.13	0.78
	1973	1.48	4.58	3.02	1.41	1.18	0.74
	1979	1.52	5.67	2.40	1.39	1.38	0.77
Standardized goods	1969	0.53	1.50	0.71	0.60	0.83	1.29
	1973	0.41	1.22	0.82	0.67	0.97	1.29
	1979	0.39	1.09	0.84	0.76	1.03	1.38
Labor-intensive	1969	0.33	14.92	0.73	1.22	1.31	0.22
	1973	0.33	1.60	0.70	0.89	1.40	0.24
	1979	0.38	1.04	0.59	0.71	0.86	0.20

B. Changes in Industry Structures: Shares of Manufacturing Value Added

		U.S.	Japan	Germany	U.K.	France	Canada
Technology-intensive	1969	0.44	0.40	0.41	0.39	0.34	0.30
	1973	0.45	0.42	0.43	0.40	0.36	0.31
	1979	0.47	0.49	0.44	0.41	0.40	0.32
Standardized goods	1969	0.38	0.45	0.45	0.41	0.54	0.52
	1973	0.38	0.42	0.45	0.41	0.51	0.51
	1979	0.37	0.42	0.43	0.40	0.48	0.50
Labor-intensive	1969	0.08	0.11	0.10	0.09	0.11	0.08
	1973	0.08	0.09	0.08	0.09	0.09	0.08
	1979	0.07	0.08	0.07	0.08	0.07	0.08

Source: Calculated from information in Tables 8 and 9, and in the case of France, from the same sources noted for other countries.

in the United States did exports grow more rapidly than imports, in large part the result of a dramatic turnaround of the textile industry.

Without exception, by 1979 all six countries had reduced the share of manufacturing value added originating in the four labor-intensive industries to 7 or 8 percent—a remarkable similarity. Furthermore, with the exception of the United Kingdom in apparel and Canada in nonfootwear leather products, the AICs decreased the share of value added originating in *each* industry. Coupled with the AICs' declining trade balances in these industries, this indicates that despite claims of excessive protection in the AICs, as a group they permitted significant adjustment away from these activities.

In the capital-intensive standardized goods-producing industries, the United States and Japan increased their absorption of imports faster than they expanded their exports, while the reverse was true for Germany, the United Kingdom, France, and Canada. As a group, though, the AICs will face heightened competition from the NICs in capital-intensive activities in coming years.

As a result of these phenomenon, the AICs are reshaping their economies in two fundamental ways.

- Rising incomes are creating larger service sectors and smaller manufacturing sectors.

- Pressure from the NICs is causing the AICs to place much greater emphasis on technology-intensive activities and exports.

Although all the AICs are moving more or less in these directions, not all are achieving the same level of success in international market competition.

Changes in the Individual AICs

In the *United States,* the competitiveness of the manufacturing sector fell from 1969 to 1979, but most of that decline occurred from 1969 to 1973. The greatest deterioration was in capital-intensive standardized goods-producing industries. This result is consistent with the decline in the abundance of capital in the United States relative to the other AICs and the NICs.

U.S. labor-intensive industries already were heavily impacted by imports when the decade began. For example, in 1969 the value of apparel imports exceeded that of exports five to one. Surprisingly, though, the average competitive performance of the labor-intensive sectors did improve, largely because of the dramatic shift of the textile industry from a net importer to a net exporter. This was achieved through substantial investment in modern machinery and an increase in the industry's capital intensity. Such experience demonstrates the fallacy of viewing an industry as permanently belonging to either of the three major industry groups and as always having the same factor requirements, when production technologies are, in fact, changing. Also, if new technology can be imported from abroad, often the case in the U.S. textile industry, R&D undertaken within the United States may be low, but the prospects for industry growth may still critically depend on the development of new products and processes.

As discussed earlier, the technology-intensive sectors made relatively greater use of both R&D scientists and engineers and other types of skilled labor (professional and technical workers). Based on comparisons for 1963 and 1980, the abundance of R&D scientists and engineers relative to other resources fell, while the opposite was true for professional and technical workers. But the first trend appears far more pronounced than the second. Hence, U.S. international competitiveness in those industries would be expected to decline, which indeed happened with alarming consistency in five industries studied.

	Export-Import Ratios: U.S. Technology-Intensive Industries				
	Transport Equipment	Electrical Machinery	Machinery, nec.	Industrial Chemicals	Other Chemicals
1969	1.17	1.57	2.77	2.70	2.82
1973	0.90	1.60	2.24	2.24	2.50
1979	0.93	1.17	2.22	2.12	2.73

Finally, from 1969 to 1979, growth rates varied considerably among the major sectors of the U.S. economy and among the industries within manufacturing, changing the relative importance of many of those industries. As in the other AICs, the technology-intensive group's share of manufacturing output increased, from 44 percent in 1969 to 47 percent in 1979. But within this group, the importance of transport equipment fell, reflecting the weakening position of automobiles. The gradual restructuring of the U.S. manufacturing sector reflects an apparent greater willingness in the United States to accept change than has been true in much of Europe.

The structure of international trade changed more in *Japan* than in any of the six AICs, with a dramatic shift toward technology-intensive activities and away from capital-intensive industries. The international competitiveness of its technology-intensive industries rose substantially, while the competitiveness of both standardized goods and labor-intensive goods fell. The rise in Japan's share of global R&D personnel and skilled labor is quite consistent with this result, as is its declining share of less skilled labor. The large increase of more than 100 percent in Japan's share of world capital stock from 1963 to 1980 might have been expected to improve the competitiveness of capital-intensive industries, such as standardized goods. However, that did not occur; we may speculate that market incentives were offset by government efforts to channel capital into technology-intensive industries. This theme will be discussed more fully in Chapter 5.

As in the U.S. case, growth rates varied considerably among Japanese industries. Like all the AICs, technology-intensive activities grew most rapidly, and hence increased in importance, while capital-intensive standardized goods industries declined. In the process, Japan's industrial structure moved closer to that of the United States. In the space of six years, the share of Japanese value added devoted to technology-intensive activities shot up so rapidly that by 1979 it had surpassed the U.S. figure in this area.

Shares of Manufacturing Value Added:
Technology-Intensive Industries

	United States	Japan
1969	0.44	0.40
1973	0.45	0.42
1979	0.47	0.49

Japan's new position vis à vis the United States in share of value added originating in the technology-intensive sector should not be totally unexpected. As cited in Chapter 2, the share of R&D personnel in the U.S. labor force actually declined over the past decade, while the number of R&D personnel in Japan grew five times more rapidly than the total Japanese labor force.

In *Germany,* areas of comparative advantage were similar to those of the United States, with its strongest competitive position in technology-intensive goods. Like the United States, German manufacturing, on the whole, lost competitiveness from 1969 to 1979. However, within manufacturing, export-import ratios declined by comparable proportions both for technology-intensive industries and for labor-intensive activities, while the competitiveness of capital-intensive standardized goods actually improved. This pattern contrasts with the U.S. situation where, as noted, the trade performance of the labor-intensive group improved with the resurgence of the textile industry, and the competitiveness of standardized goods fell. The rising competitiveness of capital-intensive goods in Germany is somewhat surprising given the decline in its share of world capital stock.

The similarity of Germany's industrial structure to that of the United States increased over the decade. The contraction of labor-intensive goods appears to have occurred more rapidly in Germany than in most countries, perhaps the result of less government intervention to promote those industries. But statistical measures of variation in growth rates across all manufacturing industries indicate that structural change was less pronounced in Germany than in Japan and even in the United States. The same was true in the United Kingdom, raising questions about the continued ability of the German and British economies to shift resources internally to take advantage of new opportunities.[1]

The competitive position of manufacturing in the *United Kingdom* declined by more than any of the other countries, although the trade balance in manufacturing was still positive in 1979. The sharpest decrease occurred in the technology-intensive group, followed by labor-intensive activities. Like Germany, the competitiveness of standardized goods rose, even though the country remained a net importer. The U.K. share of world capital stock relative to income did not fall by as much as the German share, but the greater competitiveness of capital-intensive

---

1   Over the period 1973–79, a weighted variance of the 20 industry growth rates was calculated for each country. The measure for Japan was roughly nine times the measure for Germany and the United Kingdom, while the U.S. figure was approximately twice the European values. This comparison shows that the greatest differences in growth across industries occurred in Japan, while industry growth tended to be much more uniform in Germany and the United Kingdom.

goods is still somewhat surprising. The rapid decline in the competitive position of technology-intensive goods also would not have been predicted on the basis of U.K. factor growth in skilled labor and research capability. As discussed in Chapter 5, the British experience may well be attributed to government actions that have retarded structural adjustments in its economy.

In *France,* the competitive position of manufacturing as a whole improved, with the greatest proportional increase occurring in standardized products, followed closely by technology-intensive goods. It is important to note that the trade balance in technology-intensive activities started from a position of only slight surplus in 1969. Therefore, even though its competitiveness improved, the French position only matched the British level of performance in 1979 and was substantially below the German or Japanese measures. The relatively more rapid rate of French capital formation is consistent with improved competitiveness of standardized products, while the improvement in the performance of technology-intensive industries to the same level as U.K. industries was probably more pronounced than would be expected given French growth in R&D personnel and skilled labor. This raises questions about the role of French government policies to favor technology-intensive activities over other sectors.

The change in the French industrial structure matched the pattern observed in all the AICs: technology-intensive activities expanded, standardized goods and labor-intensive goods contracted. The growth of the technology-intensive sector was substantial, but in 1979 the share of output accounted for by those industries was smaller than in any country except Canada; similarly, standardized goods remained relatively more important. French contraction in labor-intensive industries was particularly rapid, which contributed to an overall pattern of much greater structural change than in Germany or the United Kingdom. Given the more rapid rate of French economic growth noted in Chapter 2, this record supports the thesis that change, and the economic adjustments it imposes, is easier to accept in a growing economy.

The competitiveness of the three industry groups changed least in *Canada.* This is consistent with expectations based on the changes in the relative abundance of various types of capital and labor in Canada. The competitiveness of Canadian manufacturing declined very slightly over the decade, with standardized goods becoming more competitive and labor-intensive goods less so. Canada remained a net importer of technology-intensive goods. The increased competitiveness of standardized goods was attributable in part to Canada's rich endowment of natural resources in a world of growing scarcity, although Canadian investments in areas such as steel-making capacity were also important.

Canadian industrial structure also changed relatively little over the decade, but the observed shifts paralleled the patterns of other countries—the most rapid growth occurred in technology-intensive industries and the slowest growth in labor-intensive activities. However, based on a measure of the changing importance of the 20 separate industries, industry structure in Canada did not become more similar to that of the United States.

CONCLUSIONS

The results presented in this chapter suggest that underlying structural (market supply and demand) conditions indeed provide a useful basis for predicting changes in patterns of international competitiveness and industry structure, as well as resulting adjustment problems. But there are cases where expectations based on changing structural circumstances are not fulfilled, and they indicate situations in which government policies may play a decisive role—for example, in Japan and the United Kingdom, quite opposite results occurred in the technology-intensive and capital-intensive standardized goods sectors.

Due to expanded industrial capacity in the NICs and the growing capability of other AICs in high technology areas, the basis of U.S. comparative advantage has changed. The U.S. net export position in technology-intensive goods has weakened, as has its import position in capital-intensive standardized goods. Meanwhile, the United States has developed new strengths in at least one traditionally labor-intensive area (certain textile fibers and fabrics) and outside manufacturing in services. In agriculture, the U.S. comparative advantage remains strong.

As competitive pressures intensify in a traditional area of U.S. export strength, technology-intensive industries, and as U.S. exports of agricultural products and services are limited by the size of potential markets and other countries' trade-distorting practices, the United States could witness an improvement in the competitive position of manufacturing activities outside the industries currently shown in the technology-intensive group. Cost conditions in traditional labor or capital-intensive industries may change with the development and adoption of new technologies, and the competitive positions of these industries may improve, as in the case of textiles. While improved competitiveness could also result from a depreciated dollar, the United States would then pay higher prices for imports and accept a lower standard of living. Therefore, improved competitiveness should not be regarded as a goal in itself, but as a sign that greater U.S. efficiency allows U.S. producers to earn higher profits and pay higher wages.

The declining international competitiveness of U.S. manufacturing is related to changes in industry structure elsewhere. The expansion of the NICs' industrial base increased the competitive pressures faced by all the AICs; but not all have been equally adept in adjusting. Japan and the European countries expanded their availability of R&D personnel much more rapidly than the United States. Only Japan and France, though, were able to translate this into a faster rate of growth in technology-intensive industries than the United States and into an improvement in their international competitiveness.

Growth in Technology-Intensive Sectors: 1969–79	
United States	49%
Japan	107
Germany	36
United Kingdom	12
France	71
Canada	48

International Competitiveness in Technology-Intensive Sectors: Export-Import Ratios						
	U.S.	Japan	Germany	U.K.	France	Canada
1969	1.78	3.41	3.04	3.16	1.13	0.78
1979	1.52	5.67	2.40	1.38	1.38	0.77

Overall, Japan moved most rapidly to restructure its economy. To some extent, this process in Japan seems *forced* toward technology-intensive activities at the expense of capital-intensive standardized goods industries. This is almost opposite the U.K. situation, where technology-intensive industries appear unable to live up to expectations engendered by the United Kingdom's abundance of R&D scientists and engineers. Both cases generate questions about the role of government policies in influencing economic performance, which will be taken up in Part Two next.

PART TWO

The Role of Government Policies 5

As illustrated in Chapter 4, changes in underlying structural conditions in the AICs and the NICs explain many of the trends in international competitive performance of various AIC manufacturing industries. Structural factors appear to be pushing the AICs toward greater emphasis on technology-intensive activities. Yet, success in this area has not been even among the AICs, nor has it been completely consistent with expectations based on the availability of R&D capital and personnel and other factors of production. Thus, the influence of government policies and other institutional factors needs to be examined to help explain competitive performance.

Specifically, in technology-intensive industries, Japan, and to a lesser extent Germany and the United Kingdom, were expected to make the greatest gains vis à vis the United States over the 1970s. While Japan made such gains, so too did France (although the current French position is only as competitive as that of the United Kingdom). In capital-intensive standardized goods industries, Japan's competitive performance declined, and the German and U.K. positions improved, the opposite of expected developments. Such outcomes raise the following questions.

- Is Japan's policy emphasis in promoting technology-intensive activities pushing it away from capital-intensive production much more rapidly than would be expected as a result of market forces alone?

- What opportunities are being lost by producers in Germany, the United Kingdom and the United States as a result of this Japanese policy orientation? To what extent are the performances in these Western countries more the result of internal policy choices and possible misallocations?

- Are changes in U.S. policy necessary to respond to the actions of other governments?

GENERAL ASPECTS OF GOVERNMENT POLICIES

Two general types of government policies can be identified in explaining the changes in competitiveness. One set of policies is essentially macroeconomic, or designed to influence economic performance broadly; such policies are important determinants of both competitiveness internationally and industrial structure. For example, policies aimed at increasing capital formation and investment in education help determine the growth in factor endowments. Also included in this category are monetary and fiscal policies that affect interest rates, exchange rates and the rate of economic growth generally. In contrast, micro-oriented policies are designed to deal with the competitive pressures in particular industries by influencing demand and cost conditions in selected markets. Trade policies, purchasing agreements, investment controls and performance requirements, production subsidies,

R&D grants, rationalization programs, and industry cartels are examples of policies that promote particular industries. The extent to which general or macro-level factors determine changing patterns of competitiveness and industrial structure has been the focus of the preceeding chapters and will not be discussed further here. Rather, the focus is on the process through which specific industries are targeted for further assistance, and the nature of the assistance provided, even though the success of these micro-oriented policies is dependent upon macro factors operating at the same time.

In the following summary of policies adopted in Japan, Germany, the United Kingdom, France, and Canada, two major themes are traced: the government's role in promoting the expansion of particular types of industries; and the government's response when industries face severe foreign competition and are forced to contract as a result of market forces. Government actions in the United States are discussed in the next chapter.

COUNTRY SURVEYS

Japan

Japanese success in achieving high rates of growth and in becoming a world leader in the production of many manufactured products has created considerable interest in the reasons for this economic record. Because the Japanese challenge has shifted from one industry to another in an ongoing process, and the Japanese government has signaled a change of focus from capital-intensive to technology-intensive industries, the government's influence on industrial structure is of particular interest.

Historically, the government has been an important factor in Japanese economic development, and the experience under the post-World War II administrative structure is not unusual. However, an accounting of the groups responsible for determining the recent directions of industrial policy is useful in understanding the types of policies adopted and the tools used to carry them out. Two ministries have played key roles in the development and implementation of Japanese industrial policy—the Ministry of Finance (MOF) and the Ministry of International Trade and Industry (MITI).

A key function of the MOF has been to move government trust funds into selected or targeted industries through the financing offered by public corporations such as the Japan Development Bank and the Export-Import Bank. The lending priorities established have been especially important in Japan because of government efforts to keep interest rates low and then to allocate the available credit to priority industries. Even when government funds account for a small share of total financial requirements, commercial banks generally follow the government's lead. The success of Japanese firms has increased their ability to rely on retained earnings to finance expansion, even in nonpriority areas, and therefore this policy approach has become somewhat less effective. However, financial assistance through the provision of favorable export credits remains an important policy tool, particularly as Japanese exports of capital goods have risen.

Another function of the MOF is to approve tax breaks and subsidies to particular industries. In the 1960s and early 1970s, special tax provisions, such as very rapid depreciation allowances, the establishment of various loss reserves and favorable treatment of export earnings, were the more important of these two forms of assistance to priority industries. These provisions improved the cash flow position of expanding industries such as steel and automobiles. Total subsidies have represented a small share of national income. Nevertheless, Japan has continued to make strategic use of subsidies for targeted industries, products and firms in the development of its technological capabilities.

MITI has broad responsibilities that prevent it from becoming the advocate of a single industry. Examples of MITI's operating scope include recommendations regarding industries to receive government subsidies, low interest financing or special tax treatment; the promotion of mergers, where appropriate, to consolidate Japanese productive capacity or to maintain prices in depressed industries; the nature of foreign trade policy and access to the Japanese market; foreign investment and the terms on which foreign technology becomes available in Japan; and in the 1950s and 1960s, the allocation of foreign exchange to purchase imported inputs. For this broad power to be used well in accelerating the operation of market forces, MITI must have access to current, detailed information regarding industry output and prospects. Such information provides the basis for MITI to judge whether an industry is moving toward an appropriate number of producers to reach minimum cost levels of output, how research priorities should be set, and what trade policy should be pursued. The flow of information has been most consistent where strong industry trade groups exist.

Japan's policy emphasis in the 1950s and 1960s was on the development of capital-intensive activities such as shipbuilding and steel. The energy and resource constraints of the 1970s led Japanese policymakers to shift focus from these traditional capital-intensive heavy industries to the development of technology-intensive industries that would reduce dependence on foreign inputs and increase domestic productivity. Also, policymakers were forced to confront the declining competitiveness of labor-intensive industries, which faced increasing pressure from Asian NICs.

Two examples of technology-intensive industries currently being promoted by the Japanese government under the 1978 law on Extraordinary Measures for the Promotion of Specific Machinery and Information Industries are computers and robots. A key factor determining the competitiveness of these industries is the ability to fund research and development. Tax policy to encourage private research and development offers a benefit similar to a measure adopted by the United States only in 1981: a tax credit can be taken equal to 20 percent of new spending on research and development. However, such general measures are not at the heart of Japanese industrial policy, which takes a more active role in accelerating development in areas judged to be promising. Examples of recent government intervention in the computer-electronics area are support for the development of very large-scale integrated circuits and continued funding for the development of computer hardware. Financial assistance in this area was estimated to be 78.2 billion yen (U.S. $335 million) over the 1976–82 period. Although some grants are to be paid back conditional on the success of the project, repayment terms have not yet been set. Not only is the amount of government funding important, but so is the coordination of joint research on projects requiring large expenditures that may be beyond the ability of a single firm to finance. Furthermore, as pointed out in a previous study by Mutti, an even more important source of support for private industry efforts has been government procurement policies that allow development costs of domestic firms to be recovered more rapidly.[1]

In the case of robotics, government procurement is not particularly important, but several previous practices used elsewhere to promote industry demand have been adopted. Primary assistance has been provided by the Japanese Robot Leasing Company, which receives the majority of its funds as low interest loans from the Japan Development Bank, to promote sales of robots to small and medium-sized businesses. In its first year of operation, over one billion yen of leases were arranged through it. Also, tax provisions allow a firm to depreciate over one-half the cost of a robot in the year it is installed. Direct subsidies to research and development have been small so far, as an earlier program to develop an unmanned factory was dropped and a seven-year plan announced by MITI to promote highly sophisticated robots was postponed in 1982 due to budget reductions. Therefore, the eventual scale of government intervention in the industry cannot be judged very well, but the Japanese world leadership in this area is unlikely to be relinquished. High rates of investment in the economy as a whole, providing a fertile market for the adoption of new robots, represents an important demand factor favoring Japanese advances.

The data presented above indicate that Japan has been moving resources out of labor-intensive activities and that capital-intensive industries have grown slowly and declined in relative importance. In specific industries where value added and employment have dropped most rapidly, painless adjustment has not been guaranteed. Examples of government initiatives to mitigate these effects have included programs to scrap or mothball excess capacity and industry cartels that enjoy antitrust exemptions.

In recent years, statutory authority for financial assistance and industry cartels has been provided by the Structurally Depressed Industries Law of 1978, which was implemented specifically to assist long-term adjustments to changing domestic and international economic conditions. Open-hearth steel production, aluminum refining, synthetic fiber production, and shipbuilding were initially designed as depressed industries, and the law provided for future designations if specified criteria were met. Of the four industries initially designated, aluminum and steel have been least receptive to government programs to reduce capacity.

From 1978 through 1980, 10 to 20 percent of capacity in synthetic fibers was scrapped, through the purchase of 168 billion yen of excess capacity by an industry association financed with an interest free loan. Also, in 1978 a cartel was reestablished to reduce output and increase prices—a clear attempt to improve the profitability of synthetic fiber producers. While these measures do not show up as direct government subsidies to the industry, government intervention has slowed down contractions in the textile industry and reduced the losses of those forced out.

In shipbuilding, Japan's competitive position did not gradually decline; rather, the industry was hit by the collapse of the world oil tanker market in 1974. By 1979, Japanese production was only 25 percent of the 1974–75 level. This rapid contraction caused the government to channel the majority of its aid to depressed

1   John Mutti, *Taxes, Subsidies and Competitiveness Internationally* (Washington: NPA, Committee on Changing International Realities, 1982).

industries to shipbuilding rather than to textiles or other more gradually impacted industries. To reduce capacity by approximately 35 percent, the Designated Ship-building Enterprises Stabilization Association purchased nine shipyards at a cost of 36.8 billion yen, financed in part by the Japan Development Bank. In paying back these loans, 1.3 percent of the value of new orders must be paid to the asso-ciation. A recession cartel also was formed in 1979. While both industry and govern-ment recognized that demand was unlikely to recover pre-1975 levels, any restruc-turing plan has involved a negotiated balance of incentives to scrap capacity and reduce output but also to modernize within the same industry.

In summary, Japanese policy both to promote expanding industries and to assist contracting industries generally has involved government interaction with industry associations or groups of producers to set goals and to determine the responsibilities and contributions of the government and private firms. To accelerate the pace of development in particular projects, the Japanese emphasis has shifted from promoting capital-intensive industries toward targeting new technologies. This policy emphasis has the effect of moving resources into technology-intensive ac-tivities more rapidly than would be expected as a result of changes in underlying structural conditions described in Chapter 2. Hence, government intervention has increased the vulnerability to Japanese competition of U.S. and European producers in activities targeted by Japanese policymakers.

Germany

Germany has pursued a less interventionist policy than Japan and its major European competitors, France, the United Kingdom and Italy. But it has not ignored the successes achieved by economies that have adopted a more formal planning process. No official government plans are generated, but the Germans developed a process they termed *concertation*. As characterized by Franko, concertation con-sisted of "regular private consultation between the government ministries and the most senior representatives of organized business and labor, for which no official list of regular participants existed and no detailed account of actual proceedings was made public."[2] The lack of precise information regarding this process means that few answers can be given to questions of who takes the initiative and how broadly all groups are drawn into any consensus. Nevertheless, a consistent German policy appears to have developed.

In the promotion of technology-intensive sectors and the treatment of declining industries, the German approach has relied on more general policies and incentives than have France and Japan. Policies to target particular projects for support, such as a supersonic Concorde or very large-scale integrated circuits, do not represent the dominant form of assistance. In electronic data processing, a major share of available funding has been used to promote data processing generally, to generate a wider market for all producers. However, matching R&D funding has been avail-able through the Bundesministerium für Forschung and Technologie, which repre-sents a direct effort to promote the competitiveness of German technology-intensive industries, in comparison to support for basic research programs. In addition, Ger-

2   Lawrence Franko, *European Industrial Policy, Past, Present and Future* (Brussels: The Conference Board of Europe, 1980).

many has maintained the highest level of public funding of civilian research and development, as a percentage of gross domestic product, of all the European countries. An additional benefit to high technology capital goods has been active government assistance in export sales to developing countries and to the Organization of Petroleum Exporting Countries (OPEC). The nature of these policies demonstrates a strong German commitment to technology-intensive industries and suggests that growing competition with the other AICs is inevitable.

With respect to contracting industries, a common challenge to industrial countries everywhere has been the attempt to move away from labor- and capital-intensive industries such as steel, shipbuilding and apparel. Aside from shipbuilding, and more recently steel, the German Ministry of Economics has not accepted proposals to provide long-run assistance to those industries, but it has encouraged consolidation and mergers so that remaining producers may be efficient. Within the European Community (EC), Germany has pushed strongly for the elimination of steel industry subsidization and has favored more liberal textile and apparel trade than the other European countries. When aid is provided, again it often is of a general form. For instance, when Volkswagen faced difficulties in 1974, the German response was not to provide additional financing to VW, but rather to commit funds to encourage new business activities in the areas where layoffs were occurring.

However, the severity of recent recessionary conditions in Germany led to postwar high rates of bankruptcy in 1981 and 1982, and the likelihood of high unemployment rates for the decade to come, since demographic factors point to substantial increases in the labor force. As a consequence, traditional reluctance to bail out failing firms has slackened somewhat, with state and federal loans and guarantees being provided to companies with a solid outlook for recovery. Demands for government intervention in the period immediately after the worldwide slowdown in 1974 probably were muted by the ability of German producers to lay off guest workers and avoid serious unemployment of native Germans. In 1982, though, unemployment of domestic workers had risen to 7.5 percent, in spite of restrictions on new guest workers and government-sponsored repatriations of those already in Germany. The German government is pressing the EC to renegotiate a 1964 agreement that would allow free entry to Turkish workers by 1986. The government undoubtedly will face greater pressure to intervene more directly in the economy if abysmally low rates of employment growth continue, even assuming all immigration is cut off.

German producers are subject to several outside influences. Not only must they contend with Japan and the United States as technological leaders in many areas, but natural market opportunities in Europe may be blocked by nationalistic policies of countries such as France. As a consequence, the complexities faced by U.S. policymakers appear to be multiplied in Germany. To the extent that German policies can be characterized as based on general intervention, recent German trends in the competitiveness of technology-intensive industries particularly raise the question of how effective a general policy orientation can be.

United Kingdom

The United Kingdom has not pursued an industrial policy with as much government direction as Japan or France, and given its less formal approach, British goals have not clearly emerged. There has been little consensus informally to support government action, in the German vein, nor an elite bureaucracy with sufficient information to develop a comprehensive industrial plan and the power to implement it, as in France. Nevertheless, Britain's lagging growth and productivity aroused sufficient concern and interest to lead to the establishment of sector development committees and, later, sector working parties under the Industry Act of 1972. Also, small steps were taken to provide venture capital to potential growth companies through the National Enterprise Board. Yet, no comprehensive plans were formed from these various initiatives, and no consistent set of goals has emerged from the actions taken.

Much greater concern has been shown and action taken in Britain over the preservation of jobs and economic activity in their present locations. While these policies might not preclude contraction in some trade-impacted industries and expansion elsewhere, the likelihood of that match occurring is a risk British governments have been less willing to run than others; consequently, British industrial policy has been oriented to a greater extent toward maintaining the status quo. The use of funds to maintain nationalized enterprises such as British Steel and British Leyland diverts capital from successful firms and from potential growth industries. Only in the past few years have sharp capacity reductions in the steel industry been accepted as national policy, and the process of contraction continues to be an expensive one.

In the 1970s, British industrial assistance programs were not nearly as selective as French or German efforts, providing instead various forms of aid to a much larger number of separate industries. Franko cites the reported goals of all 40 sector working parties to stabilize or reduce import penetration, a sign of little willingness to reallocate resources as a consequence of pursuing gains from specialization. Britain's effective corporate tax rates are relatively low, so that industry-specific incentives through the tax code are not especially strong. Promotion of particular technology-intensive industries comes from steps such as R&D grants or government equity funding of new enterprises. However, project funding is not the only relevant factor. British expenditures on R&D as a share of GNP exceed those in France, but Britain's competitive performance has declined while the French position has improved. Inadequate efforts to commercialize scientific innovations have been a self-recognized British weakness.

As an example of British support of high technology industries such as computers, the government did assume equity ownership of 10 percent in International Computers Limited in 1968, and the ownership share was expanded to 24.5 percent before the government interest was sold in 1979. R&D grants consistently were made to ICL, and government procurement policies provided an even larger financial subsidy, perhaps equivalent to 9 percent of sales. Yet, ICL's market share fell over the 1970s, and the company was on the verge of bankruptcy by 1981. The Thatcher government blocked any joint venture proposals by American firms and provided a $420 million loan guarantee to ICL, a nationalistic policy reminiscent of de Gaulle's approach in France. Also, this attitude stands in contrast to the German acceptance of joint ventures with Japanese firms to strengthen their competitive position internationally.

In summary, British policy has put relatively greater emphasis on assistance to declining industries and has found that efforts to restructure and modernize those industries are not cheap. Steps to promote technology-intensive industries and to accelerate commercial applications of basic research findings have not been as extensive. These factors in part explain why British competitiveness in technology-intensive industries has declined, in contrast to predictions based on the structural considerations described in Chapter 2. However, the British record undoubtedly has been affected by many factors other than government industrial policy, such as labor-management relations, the system of rewards to entrepreneurship, the existence of venture capital markets, the nature of bank lending policies, and the attractiveness of the United Kingdom as a host country for operations by foreigners.

France

The success of French industrial policy in the 1950s and early 1960s caused other European countries to consider similar measures as a means of spurring manufactured output. The actual tools to be used in implementing French policy appear to be changing somewhat under the current socialistic government of François Mitterrand, but stated national goals are not that different. Two priorities of French industrial strategy have been the development of an independent military capability and the encouragement of energy production, including nuclear power generation. A related goal has been the promotion of technology-intensive industries. The French practice of clearly designating industries to be promoted, restructured or contracted is quite unique relative to the less explicit policies of other Western industrial countries.

The French process is referred to as *indicative planning,* and through the early 1960s a series of five-year plans represented a comprehensive approach toward promoting growth industries and encouraging mergers and consolidation in declining industries. The extent of intervention exceeded that of other European governments, and the capability of the bureaucracy that conceptualized those plans also was not matched elsewhere in Europe. Some French choices in industrial policy can be attributed to nationalistic motives, such as its independent defense capability or development of the supersonic Concorde, while other choices, such as the promotion of nuclear power, have been a consequence of the lack of alternative French energy resources. However, not all post-de Gaulle choices necessarily represent a policy of picking winners. Substantial government assistance was provided in the de facto nationalization of the steel industry in 1978. The favorable financing of foreign acquisitions by Peugeot and government-owned Renault may or may not result in profitable operations. Also, the commercial payoff to expertise in nuclear power is far from guaranteed in international markets. The low budgetary cost of trade protection undoubtedly has increased its attraction as an alternative policy instrument, and France has been an aggressive voice within Europe pushing for limitations on imports of apparel and textiles, steel and automobiles.

Nevertheless, Franko claims that the main focus of French industrial policy remains the promotion of technology-intensive industries rather than maintaining the status quo. Examples of this direction are continued large support for nuclear power, aircraft production and export financing (an important aid in the sale of high technology capital goods). However, the nationalizations carried out by the Mitterrand government in 1981 and 1982 included major producers in technology-intensive industries. Government officials justify this approach on the grounds that government ownership will allow greater risk-taking without the concern of conservative stockholders. Direct state intervention is seen as necessary to counteract the flow of nearly half of French savings into real estate over the past decade, instead of job-creating investment. The French anticipate being able to promote technology-intensive industries, possibly involving joint ventures with American firms, by adopting the Japanese practice of using a captive home market as a base from which to develop an export ability. The large French domestic market would seem to give them a stronger bargaining position in this regard than the Canadians, for example. The French government also has stated its intention to increase government support for R&D expenditures to a level exceeding any other European country. In 1982, 14 priority projects in the electronics area were identified, such as computer-aided design and speech synthesis. The way these projects will be funded has not been specified, nor is it clear whether this project-oriented approach represents a retreat from more general forms of assistance introduced under Giscard d'Estaing that still allowed market forces to determine which producers among several might be successful. Also, the reimposition of price controls in 1982 raises questions over the future flexibility of business in France.

Canada

Canadian industrial policy has in part evolved in an attempt to avoid overreliance on natural resource extraction and to cope with high levels of foreign investment. Thus, its industrial policy represents a reaction to circumstances quite different from the Japanese case. A study by Morici, Smith and Lea identifies the following common industrial goals that can be inferred from Canadian government actions: (1) to derive greater national benefit and greater value added within Canada from its natural resource base; (2) to rationalize production within manufacturing industries to meet the intensified international competition that is following the Tokyo Round tariff reductions; (3) to promote greater Canadian participation in high technology industries including more indigenous R&D; and (4) to ensure that the benefits of economic progress are shared by the various geographic regions within Canada.[3]

Over the past decade, both the federal and provincial governments have taken more activist roles in pursuing these goals. Institutionally, there has been considerable change as well. At present, the Priorities and Planning Committee of the Cabinet, together with the Prime Minister, set overall expenditure levels for the entire government and individual policy sectors. They also determine the general tone for economic development policy. With respect to the implementation of industrial policy, primary responsibility rests with the Cabinet Committee on Economic and Regional Development. The cohesiveness of government-business relationships found in Japan is not replicated here, but Canada's administrative structure provides the basis for evaluating industrial policies and recommending modifications when appropriate.

The Canadian government has taken broad measures to benefit the entire manufacturing sector, such as setting a corporate income tax rate of 40 percent in manufacturing industries versus 46 percent in the economy as a whole, allow-

---

3   Peter Morici, Arthur J.R. Smith and Sperry Lea, *Canadian Industrial Policy* (Washington: NPA, 1982), p. 24.

ing machinery and equipment used in processing and manufacturing to be written off in two years, and providing investment tax credits for activity in depressed regions of the country. Canadian government estimates of the tax revenue foregone as a result of these program provisions were $1.3 billion in 1980.

While this assistance provides an incentive to shift resources into manufacturing and helps avoid the stereotyped role of Canadian producers as "hewers of wood and drawers of water," it is not nearly as focused as the more activist goals listed above would require. Instead, the achievement of those goals has involved greater reliance on other incentive programs rather than the manipulation of the tax code to benefit particular industries, a contrast to the Japanese approach. The Enterprise Development Program replaced several independent, industry-specific measures, which primarily provided loans and guarantees within the manufacturing sector. The potential to favor particular industries appears present here, as well as through the Federal Business Development Bank and Small Business Loans Program, which together accounted for over $2.3 billion in loans and guarantees in 1980. However, in terms of dollar commitments, the Canadian Development Corporation investments in petrochemicals, mining and oil and gas have accounted for even larger financial involvement.[4]

An important tool in shaping Canadian industrial policy that may be politically attractive, because it does not have the same government budgetary implications as direct subsidies and tax breaks, is regulation of direct foreign investment in Canada. Since the mid 1960s, the Canadian government has formulated expectations concerning multinational corporation actions with respect to product specialization, exporting, domestic procurement, R&D performance domestically, and the "Canadianization" of management. This set of expectations became more explicit and enforceable under the Foreign Investment Review Agency established in 1973 to review most new foreign investments and acquisitions. Morici et al. note that initial decisions by FIRA seemed to take more account of domestic employment and output impacts than export performance or R&D capability; however, more recent policy statements suggest greater emphasis will be placed on the latter criteria. Also, in the energy sector, majority Canadian ownership appears to be the new goal, regardless of foreign firms' performance. Multinational corporations undoubtedly are used to the situation of changing rules of operation, based on their experience in other countries, and Canadian action in this regard is not surprising.

However, to be effective, Canadian implementation will have to be pragmatic. Its greatest strength and ability to extract concessions from multinationals would seem to rest in industries exploiting Canadian natural resources or those acting as suppliers to resource development projects. Even here, though, the emergence of worldwide excess supplies in several natural resource industries in the early 1980s demonstrates that the national interest may change rapidly. With regard to other policies, an ability to enforce worldwide export mandates on the Canadian operations of multinationals may be limited unless offsetting benefits are offered, such

4   The CDC is a public-private corporation established in 1971 in part out of concern for the level of foreign ownership in the Canadian economy. It has a mandate to invest in industries that have long-range development prospects, increase the level of domestic resource processing, possess a high technological base, and have good potential for increasing Canadian presence in international markets.

as the opportunity to make sales in a Canadian market still protected by government and Crown corporation procurement policies. The opportunity to serve the Canadian domestic market is not as big a bargaining chip as it would be in the case of more populous countries, especially if provincial policies and preferences result in the Balkanization of the Canadian market, a possibility noted by Morici et al. In addition, if the government is successful in attracting more R&D activity to Canada, it must then face questions with respect to the further commitment of firms to use that technology in Canadian production versus transferring it elsewhere. Therefore, while efforts to influence multinationals represent a feasible way to promote certain types of activity and move Canada toward some of its industrial goals, several unresolved questions remain regarding the execution of that policy.

With respect to declining industries, such as footwear, textiles and apparel, the Canadian government has established an assistance program for those industries alone and also provides support payments for workers laid off. Expenditures on this program in the 1979–80 fiscal year were $3.3 million. The Canadian government has taken advantage of the Multi-Fiber Arrangement governing trade in textiles and apparel to negotiate more stringent bilateral limits on imports, a step other industrial countries have taken to reduce the scope of layoffs. The Canadian textile and apparel industries have not contracted as much as the same sectors in the other AICs. This issue is particularly sensitive in Canada due to a more than proportional concentration of those industries in Quebec. These examples demonstrate a continued commitment to assisting impacted workers, which stands in contrast to the drastic cutback of Trade Adjustment Assistance in the United States. However, the currently limited Canadian plan does not provide a clearly successful model to be applied in making the many adjustments within the Canadian manufacturing sector that are likely to result from Tokyo Round multilateral trade concessions.

CONCLUSIONS

The industrial policies of the other AICs demonstrate a variety of attitudes toward promoting change and encouraging particular industries. In Japan, the government has taken an especially active role in influencing economic development, but this involvement has not resulted in a permanent commitment to a fixed group of industries. Rather, Japanese priorities have shifted several times, and in the past decade were designed to reduce Japanese dependence on heavy industry and to promote the development of technology-intensive industries. Japan's performance in international markets suggests that its policies can be quite successful in achieving those goals. Semiconductors and numerically controlled machine tools are examples of opportunities recently lost by U.S. producers as a result of Japanese targeting of particular industries for accelerated product innovation and development. Government assistance to Japanese producers may not eliminate foreign competitors, but it reduces the payoff to innovations by others.

Although technology-intensive industries grew at above average rates in all countries studied, their competitiveness internationally did not match Japan's rapid expansion. Different government strategies and priorities influenced the results significantly. British policies focused to a greater extent on assisting traditional industries, thereby diverting resources from technology-intensive activities. German policies were less project-specific than in Japan. Over the past decade, Germany lost its position as the largest exporter of technology-intensive products; this result appears attributable not only to Japanese competition, but also to the nature of policies pursued by its European partners, especially France, whose competitiveness increased substantially, although from a lower initial base. Finally, Canada's efforts to overcome its traditional position as a net importer of technology-intensive products were linked to incentives and conditions attached to foreign investment plans in its economy. Even if successful, Canada's unique circumstances imply that its experiences do not offer a general model for the United States.

This brief summary of foreign government intervention forms the basis for the concluding chapter of the study, which outlines a broad set of issues facing the United States. Just as foreign governments have promoted some industries at the expense of others, U.S. government actions have different impacts across industries, whether or not decisionmakers recognize them. The final chapter describes past U.S. policies, and the incentives they created, and presents three alternative approaches to be considered in formulating more effective U.S. policies.

Issues Facing the United States 6

As the U.S. economy recovers from the 1981–82 recession, the unemployment and hardships experienced by workers in many basic industries, such as steel, nonferrous metals and automobiles, cannot be expected to disappear. In contrast to earlier postwar recessions when generally slack demand was the cause of layoffs in those industries, the structure of the U.S. economy has shifted over the past decade and the U.S. competitive position has changed.

Competition from the NICs in activities using large amounts of unskilled labor has spread to more capital-intensive industries producing standardized products, and this trend will continue. The pressures on U.S. producers will increase as other AICs attempt to maintain employment in these same basic industries, since excess capacity and closed markets abroad shift NIC exports and structural adjustment problems onto the United States. In addition, changes in technology and consumer preferences may weaken demand for some of these products, further exacerbating adjustment problems in the industries. For example, higher energy prices have shifted consumer demand toward smaller cars and fewer miles driven, which has reduced the demand for steel and other basic materials and cut automobile purchases. Breakthroughs in electronics have reduced the potential demand for copper. New, expensive electronic devices such as home computers and VCRs now compete for consumer expenditures against other more traditional durable goods.

Whether output in these traditional manufacturing activities continues to grow will depend significantly upon how effectively they modernize their capital facilities and take other steps to improve productivity—e.g., improving labor management relations, upgrading labor skills, altering work rules, increasing worker and management commitments to quality production, and developing more efficient management structures. While these steps do not guarantee that employment will expand, or that an industry can shift from a net import to a net export position, they are necessary to avoid more drastic declines in competitiveness and employment.

Even under the most optimistic assumptions, the challenge of generating adequate employment opportunities for workers displaced from traditional manufacturing activities is an important national policy question. This consideration, along with the concern of maintaining an adequate industrial capacity for national defense purposes, will remain important issues in the continuing debate over what kind of industrial development policies the nation should pursue.

In many technology-intensive industries, an area of traditional strength, the United States is confronted by growing competition. In machine tools, computers, construction machinery, and aerospace, U.S. firms are facing concerted Japanese and European challenges. Foreign capabilities have expanded as R&D spending and personnel have increased. Further, this spending has not been concentrated in basic research, but rather in commercially oriented projects, particularly the development of improved process technologies. In areas where the U.S. position has been dominant, foreign governments have been particularly prone to adopt development subsidies and other nonmarket strategies to improve the ability of their domestic firms to erode the U.S. international market share.

While foreign industrial policies have been important, the U.S. government, at various times, has taken initiatives to assist industries and workers, although these have not been pursued within the context of a specific planning process and have been ad hoc. Moreover, as in other countries, some U.S. initiatives—outside the realm of policies designed to assist firms and workers—have had negative effects on U.S. competitiveness and employment. Examples in the United States include the administration of U.S. regulatory and antitrust policies during the 1960s and 1970s. Also, restrictions on U.S. exports to achieve foreign policy objectives did not always have the desired results, but cost U.S. firms and workers important opportunities. Similarly, the configuration of fiscal and monetary policies that have given the United States record interest rates and an overvalued dollar is costing America exports and jobs.

How should the U.S. government cope with foreign and domestic initiatives that affect U.S. competitiveness? To address this issue, this chapter begins with a selective survey of U.S. policies, comparable to those of the other AICs described in Chapter 5. This summary of past U.S. activities, together with examples of successful and unsuccessful intervention in other countries, is then used to set out three broad alternative courses of action open to the United States in the 1980s. The options described here should not be interpreted as mutually exclusive, and in fact current and future policies may include elements described under each of the three headings. However, the three alternatives show that clear choices must be made in establishing economic and social priorities in the United States and in determining the proper role of government in achieving them.

A SELECTIVE SURVEY OF U.S. POLICIES

In peacetime, the United States has never relied on extensive planning processes or developed a procedure to coordinate separate policies that affect the prospects for growth and competitiveness of U.S. manufacturing industries; consequently, the United States does not have an explicit industrial policy. Comprehensive planning and listing of industries and projects to be promoted, as well as those to be discouraged, are practiced by the French and Japanese, but to date have not been adopted in the United States.

In the case of trade-impacted industries, U.S. policy generally has been formulated on a sectoral basis with each affected industry considered separately. This is particularly true now that more uniform policies applicable to all industries, such as Trade Adjustment Assistance, are being de-emphasized. The demise of TAA can be traced to its greater usage after the revised eligibility standards of the Trade Act of 1974 were implemented and its budgetary cost rose dramatically. Voluntary trade restraints, such as the 1981 automobile agreement with Japan, are representative of a common policy approach adopted in many other countries to avoid federal budget expenditures.

The variety of policies pursued in the steel industry over the past decade provides a good basis for analyzing the U.S. response to trade-impacted industries. Although action was taken in 1969 to negotiate voluntary export restraints with the EC and Japan, a more recent approach is represented by the Trigger Price Mechanism, imposed in 1978 to stem a surge of imports that often sold at prices well below average total cost of production. The TPM represented a step short of quantitative restrictions; it also maintained some market discipline by tying minimum import prices to the costs of the most efficient producer in the world, Japan. Because sales below the trigger price caused an accelerated dumping investigation to be initiated, the payoff to foreign price cutting was reduced, and U.S. steel production, prices and profits increased. Perhaps no one in the industry viewed the Trigger Price Mechanism as significantly improving the long-run outlook for U.S. producers, though, because investment in the industry did not rise to the same extent. Instead, firms continued to diversify out of steel, the prime example being U.S. Steel's purchase of Marathon Oil.

Diversification itself may not be inadvisable, and in fact may represent a reasonable outcome from the viewpoint of the affected firms if the prospects are poor that major new facilities in the United States actually can be competitive with those built elsewhere in the world. However, diversification usually does little to reemploy workers displaced by import competition or to ease the adjustments they and their communities must bear. All of this raises questions with respect to the government's goals in providing special assistance. Reich frames this issue in terms of the *accountability* of sectors receiving special assistance.[1] Essentially, if explicit goals are not formulated when a policy is adopted, then the firms and workers benefiting from them cannot be held accountable for doing their share to accomplish those goals.

Another aspect of government intervention in the steel industry was the formation of a tripartite government-business-labor committee to provide a forum for developing U.S. policy. The OECD also created a committee to deal with the situation internationally, a recognition by participating countries that government actions were highly interdependent. Both committees subsequently were dissolved, although contentious trade issues still remained.

In 1981, countervailing duty (CVD) cases were brought against several European carbon steel producers who benefited from government subsidies. These cases were brought under the new code agreed to in the 1979 Multilateral Trade Negotiations, which allowed action to be taken against subsidies to domestic producers and not just those to exporters. The duties subsequently assessed by the U.S. Commerce Department were never imposed, though, as political interests in Europe and the United States led to negotiated voluntary export restraints in 1982 instead. Another recent CVD case involved subsidized sales of Canadian subway cars to the United States. Although a ruling against the Canadian producer, Bombardier, was issued, the American producer, Budd, withdrew its complaint, and several other parties were ruled ineligible to pursue the case. In neither situation, then, has there been a chance to judge the effectiveness of remedies available under the new CVD code.

Turning to policies most relevant to export industries, a mixed picture also emerges. U.S. export credit financing through the Export-Import Bank became more aggressive in 1982, particularly with respect to the length of time for which credits were made available. A result of this stance was the renegotiation among OECD

---

1   Robert Reich, "Making Industrial Policy," *Foreign Affairs* (Spring 1982), pp. 852–881.

countries of minimum interest rates to be offered on export sales. Separately, in 1981, an accord with European countries was reached on allowable terms of finance for commercial aircraft sales. In 1983, the United States has used subsidized export sales of agricultural products as an apparent bargaining ploy to force negotiations with the European Community over its agricultural policy. Thus, greater U.S. intervention may not signal a greater long-run commitment to increased levels of U.S. export subsidization, but rather a strategic attempt to negotiate reduced intervention by foreign governments.

Of increasing importance in recent years has been government intervention to prohibit or restrict U.S. export sales. In the case of agriculture, exports have been restricted to keep domestic prices down, as in the soybean embargo in 1973, or to serve foreign policy objectives, as in the limitation of U.S. grain sales to the Soviet Union. The prohibition of sales of high technology goods by U.S. firms or their affiliates for construction of the Soviet gas pipeline also demonstrates the importance of foreign policy considerations in shaping U.S. export prospects.

A more general issue with respect to technology-intensive industries is government support of R&D. Figures cited by Franko regarding government support of civilian R&D as a share of gross national product show the United States has fallen to the level of France and the United Kingdom, a figure less than German or Japanese support.[2] Since U.S. or foreign tax credits to support commercial R&D are not reflected in those figures, the smaller government role before 1982 is even greater than appears from this comparison. With respect to total public and private civilian R&D spending, U.S. outlays as a share of GNP have risen slightly from the mid 1960s, although the absolute percentage and the rate of increase still have been smaller than for Germany and Japan. Comparable GNP shares in France and the United Kingdom initially were greater than in the United States, but by 1979 were smaller. This lag behind the German and Japanese expenditures mirrors the pattern found under the more general measure of R&D personnel cited earlier.

An important part of U.S. support for R&D is government expenditures for defense and space related projects. But, as Reich emphasizes, the way in which this research is conducted tends to reduce the potential payoff in commercial applications. The Defense Department's preference to sign sole source contracts, to deal with the same firms over time and to fund projects on a cost-plus basis often eliminates incentives for efficiency that are necessary in commercial production. Nevertheless, the U.S. commercial aircraft and aerospace industries and computer and electronics industries have benefited from the strong domestic market created by U.S. government procurement even if these benefits have not been as great as the absolute dollars spent would indicate.

In general, U.S. policy appears less interventionist than in other countries. When programs are adopted, they tend to be considered in a relatively narrow context and not as part of a well articulated plan or view of a preferred industrial structure. U.S. trade intervention has been far from uniform, with restrictive action most likely to be taken in the case of industries where employment consequences are large.

2   Lawrence Franko, *European Industrial Policy, Past, Present and Future* (Brussels: The Conference Board of Europe, 1980).

ALTERNATIVE POLICY APPROACHES

This concluding portion of the study describes three alternative roles for the U.S. government regarding the way its policies to affect international competitiveness and industrial structure might be designed. The alternatives are referred to here as a market-oriented approach based on minimal government intervention; acceptance of selective government intervention if carried out more effectively; and industrial policy planning. Rather than prescribe a single approach, this discussion illustrates the diversity of views from which any U.S. policy must be formed and highlights some of the key questions that future policies will have to address. The categorizations presented here do not include all possible positions, nor are the separate policy tools described and questions raised in each section of relevance only to advocates of that particular approach. Still other approaches and different issues undoubtedly will develop as competitive conditions change over time. Nevertheless, the present discussion provides a useful starting point.

Market-oriented Approach

One approach toward improving U.S. competitiveness internationally would be to rely more on market forces to allocate resources in the economy. This would imply a level of government intervention limited to situations where markets are unable to work efficiently due to a lack of competition, inadequate information, externalities, or other outside forces such as the trade-distorting practices of other countries.

This approach implies an agnostic view with respect to any ideal industrial structure and does not require any government apparatus or decisionmaking hierarchy to determine explicit priorities over which industries would be promoted and which should be restructured and contracted. In terms of two themes identified in Chapter 5, the nature of policies to retard the decline of some industries and policies to accelerate the growth of others, a stance in favor of minimal government intervention implies little should be done in either case. According to this view, policies to restrict the growth of imports should be reduced because they force higher costs on U.S. buyers of those goods, and U.S. firms have less incentive to produce efficiently and sell competitively. Trade restrictions merely postpone the shifting of resources to sectors of the economy where they can be used more effectively. Producers in the export sectors of the economy are especially penalized by having their costs driven up, not only for imported inputs but also for other inputs used in producing domestic substitutes. By this view, voluntary export restraints on Japanese automobiles simply reduce the overall efficiency of the U.S. economy while transferring income to those in the protected sectors. Even programs such as Trade Adjustment Assistance, which provide compensation to those displaced by imports, are regarded as inefficient in promoting adjustment since workers in the past have tended to collect TAA payments while waiting to be recalled to their original jobs in the impacted industry.

Similarly, according to the market-oriented position, special tax breaks or targeted financial subsidies to export producers are generally not warranted. Pushing more resources into export·production than would be called for on the basis of market incentives merely reduces the efficiency of the U.S. economy and drives up costs in other sectors. A similar conclusion was reached by McCulloch, who pointed out that subsidies to commercial R&D are justified only when other market distortions exist, such as programs that already skew the allocation of resources toward other sectors of the economy (as in the case of tax breaks for residential housing), or when there are important spillovers from R&D activity in promoting greater productivity and faster growth throughout the economy.[3]

Minimal government intervention certainly need not imply no intervention, especially with respect to trade policy. World economic efficiency falls when foreign government policies distort the pattern of international trade, and more efficient resource allocation calls for aggressive enforcement of U.S. trade laws and rights under the GATT Articles of Agreement. Examples of possible U.S. policy responses are the imposition of countervailing duties on subsidized imports or the application of Section 301 of the Trade Act of 1974 to offset unfair trade practices abroad.

While the market-oriented case for government action is fairly clear cut when foreigners explicitly subsidize products exported to the United States or when they discriminate against U.S. goods, critical policy issues do arise when other countries' policies affect U.S. trade prospects, output and employment less directly.

For example, how should the United States handle the deflection of NIC or Japanese exports to the United States when other major markets such as the European Community limit their imports? When European nations restrict Japanese automobile sales or provide infant industry protection to their own semiconductor producers, foreign production is deflected to the U.S. market; the intensified competition and lower profit margins faced by U.S. producers are the result of government intervention elsewhere. To what extent does an advocate of market solutions support U.S. government intervention to offset such nonmarket influences?

Similarly, foreign government efforts to establish viable domestic producers challenge U.S. technological leaders in industries such as aerospace and computers and reduce U.S. producers' share of the world market. Since a CVD policy only affects imports into the United States, are other steps to assist U.S. firms justified?

Improved Limited Intervention

The United States has not pursued the market-oriented approach outlined above. Measures taken to reduce adjustment costs in trade-impacted sectors and to assist export-oriented activities have been adopted for reasons other than the correction of market failures. Moreover, U.S. government involvement has been somewhat uncoordinated and ad hoc. Goals for assisted activities and industries have usually not been stated explicitly; hence, government policies have often generated results inconsistent with the expectations of labor, management, government officials, or the general public. To the extent that common goals for these policies exist, an alternative response to the deteriorating U.S. competitive position internationally might rest on a similar level of government intervention, but attempt to redesign the actual policy tools used to better take account of the sometimes perverse market incentives created.

In this view, current examples of intervention through orderly marketing agree-

---

3   Rachel McCulloch, *Research and Development as a Determinant of U.S. International Competitiveness* (Washington: NPA, Committee on Changing International Realities, 1978).

ments, voluntary export restraints, adjustment assistance programs, and export promotion can be legitimate policy steps. Such policies avoid drastic shifts in production, in the demand for different types of labor skills, and in income distribution that would occur in the absence of government intervention. Also, they reduce the rate of structural adjustments and consequent economic hardships that would occur otherwise. To the advocates of such an approach, the benefits of moderating income losses and other social costs imposed by dramatic changes in competitiveness may be just as important as the potential increases in economic efficiency achieved by more rapid structural change. A tradeoff between social goals and economic efficiency considerations exists, and the choice among the basic government policy responses sketched here will depend in part upon choices with respect to this tradeoff.

Efforts to assist import-competing firms and workers and provisions for export promotion need not be regarded simply as policies motivated by political expediency as opposed to economic standards. They also can be justified on economic efficiency grounds in cases of structural unemployment and when greater productivity results from new investments and increased economies of scale achieved by assisted firms. For such an argument to hold, though, other distortions must exist in the economy that prevent potentially successful enterprises from raising necessary capital to carry out such modernizations or that increase the national payoff from promoting domestic output rather than relying upon cheaper imports.

Whether government intervention is selected to respond to domestic distortions, to offset unfair trade practices abroad or to achieve social goals, such practices do not necessarily encourage gradual adjustment to changing international realities. In this respect, the label "improved limited intervention" suggests that the nature of government policies could be altered to better ensure that the economy does not remain locked into inefficient production patterns and instead adjusts toward greater economic efficiency. At the same time, the "limited" label implies that no comprehensive design for the economy as a whole need be established, but that actions taken in individual sectors could be developed on a different basis than currently. This view is based on the concept of accountability mentioned previously and assumes that future intervention will rest on a clear statement of the goals and responsibilities of those who benefit from government action.

For example, in the steel case discussed earlier, the following sorts of questions might be raised. If policies of trade restriction generate higher cash flows for import-impacted firms, are any obligations imposed on those firms regarding scrapping excess capacity, investing in modern facilities or retraining and relocating displaced workers? In diversified firms, job transfers may be a feasible form of adjustment, and in fact government funds made available to declining industries in Japan often carry an obligation to arrange worker retraining and relocation. Should government trade intervention, the relaxation of other government regulations or the approval of certain mergers in an industry be treated comparably in the United States, as a form of aid with strings attached?

In addition, if import protection or other government assistance is provided, do labor groups accept any obligations with respect to work rule changes or wage settlements that will affect the industry's competitiveness? Recent contract renegotiations in the auto, steel and aluminum industries have demonstrated labor flexibility under extreme conditions when the health of the industry clearly was in jeopardy. With shorter contract cycles and more continual sharing of information between labor and management, would layoffs be reduced in U.S. manufacturing industries? Would less regularity in wage changes be preferable to greater certainty over employment? Even in the current renegotiations, the way in which blue-collar workers, white-collar workers and executives are expected to share in the burdens of adjustment has not been treated in a straightforward, coordinated fashion.

Because explicit agreements seldom are made in conjunction with government intervention, no basis exists for holding a party accountable if the action does not seem to match implicit but unstated objectives. Protection might allow a breathing space in which the industry can generate the profits to adopt new technologies, modernize and improve its competitiveness internationally. The experience of portions of the U.S. textile industry cited earlier might fall in this category, although employment has fallen in the industry. Because goals might be formulated in terms of improved competitiveness, rising output or increased employment in the industry, the consistency of these alternative standards should be assessed before the fact.

To determine the explicit goals and responsibilities for an industry requiring special assistance implies a different sort of decisionmaking process than exists at present. The tripartite government-management-labor committee formed in the case of the steel industry suggests one of several possible mechanisms, while the operation of the government loan board in the case of federal assistance to Chrysler represents a more limited model. For such committees to be successful requires an interchange of information that usually does not occur among competitors or between representatives of labor, management and the government. Traditional restrictions such as antitrust laws may need to be changed to carry out some of the policies designed to improve the competitiveness of an industry. Also, a more activist role by the industry committees in collecting information on policies and practices elsewhere may be necessary to anticipate more carefully the competitive situation that will be faced in the future and to determine the most appropriate reaction by the U.S. industry and government. One potential drawback of industry-oriented approaches is that little attention need be paid to any repercussions on other industries; consequently, few counterweights are built into this ad hoc approach. Also, nothing would prevent a group of industry committees from formulating industry goals and policies separately that in the aggregate might largely cancel each other out or that focus on only limited interests. Stated somewhat more directly, it is impossible to provide above average assistance to all sectors of the economy.

Industrial Policy Planning

The third general policy response summarized here suggests a greater departure from past U.S. practices motivated largely by a different view of the nature of international competition today. While no simple and commonly accepted definition of industrial policy exists, in this study it refers to a government effort to establish a coordinated set of goals and expectations for separate industries and to the formulation of government and private actions to achieve them. The first two alternatives described above result in a market outcome that encourages some industries and discourages others. Industrial policy planning is used here to signify an explicit attempt to assess the desirability of the pattern of production and competitiveness that results. Advocates of this approach, therefore, must accept that greater attention be paid to the interrelated nature of government policies in separate industries. Also, the way in which macro-level policies have different effects on individual industries must be taken into account.

An important motivation of those advocating broader U.S. government intervention in the market process is the belief that intervention by other countries to promote industries within their economies has left U.S. producers responding to the whims and preferences of other governments. U.S. businesses face greater competition in industries that foreign governments choose to favor and face less competition in industries passed over by foreign governments. As a consequence, U.S. industrial structure is shaped by foreign governments, and its evolution in continually making the residual adjustments forced by others may bear little relationship to what a free market solution would generate or to a pattern judged desirable by Americans generally.

A strategic implication of this trend is that U.S. industrial capacity may shrink to the point where domestic production in some critical areas no longer is sufficient to meet U.S. military needs. For example, Reich has expressed the view that it may become necessary, for security reasons, for the U.S. government to provide incentives for the construction of two large integrated steel mills, each with a six million ton capacity.[4] Also, changes in the industrial structure are altering the types of employment opportunities available to American workers, potentially resulting in a more polarized society with low skilled workers and highly skilled workers, but few in between. In this context, more effective retraining programs may not be sufficient to result in a desirable structure of jobs.

This view implies that if the U.S. policy response is to be more than a mere reaction to market incentives that are distorted by large-scale intervention of foreign governments, then a greater effort must be made to evaluate how the U.S. economy is evolving and in what direction it should move instead. To carry out such an analysis, examples of successful industrial policy planning suggest the importance of a policymaking body that has a larger constituency than a single industry. For example, the Japanese experience with MITI is a situation where priorities among industries can be set and paralysis attributable to conflicts among the competing demands of equally weighted industries can be avoided. Evaluating possible structures to be adopted in the United States is beyond the scope of this overview, but the need for an oversight group would seem to distinguish industrial policy planning from the ad hoc policy improvements discussed previously. Accountability would be no less a part of industrial policy planning. However, the formulation of goals and expectations for beneficiaries of government aid would likely be a more consistent process across industries if a more systematic approach were enforced by an oversight group than if such a process were initiated anew in each industry.

Simultaneously, a better understanding of the scope of policies pursued in other countries is necessary. To combat the situation in which the United States becomes the residual party making costly economic and social adjustments in reaction to the policies of others, a very active trade policy would be necessary. A greater role for the government in initiating and actually implementing the rulings reached in countervailing duty and antidumping cases would reduce the pressures faced by U.S. import-competing industries as a result of foreign practices. Greater

---

4   Robert Reich, "The Next American Frontier," *The Atlantic Monthly* (April 1983), p. 104.

use of Section 301 of the Trade Act of 1974 would reduce the impact of foreign government practices on U.S. exporters. Perhaps this more aggressive trade policy would force some form of international agreement regarding the way in which all nations must take into account the interests of other nations in formulating their domestic industrial policies. That possible result should not be assumed, though, and the pursuit of this approach would imply a much larger commitment of resources to the actual conduct of trade policy than is currently the case.

CONCLUSIONS

Although these stylized representations of three different policy alternatives are too brief to give a full hearing to the merits or drawbacks of each approach, they highlight important types of policy questions facing the United States. Some of the questions are factual.

- Granted that U.S. import-competing and export industries have been affected by policies adopted by other countries to promote particular industries within their economies, how often do the consequences exceed a threshhold level that would warrant a U.S. response?

- Do international agreements provide a sufficient basis for U.S. trade policy to protect U.S. producers from foreign government practices?

- Have foreign countries accelerated their targeting of particular industries in recent years?

- Have U.S. trade patterns been characterized to an increasing extent by unpredictable surges in import penetration or the sudden loss of traditional export markets? In such cases are U.S. producers forced to contract output and employment, spreading adjustments over increasingly short time periods?

- At what cost to U.S. workers and firms is production being shifted out of industries impacted by foreign intervention and into other activities?

- What manpower policies would assist workers to adjust to structural change imposed by intensified international competition, and what would be their budgetary costs?

Some questions require more subjective answers or a national political consensus.

- To what extent should government policies sacrifice economic efficiency to guarantee that the cost of adjustment in the economy is not borne disproportionately by trade-impacted producers and workers?

- Does one type of industry structure give a more desirable distribution of benefits individually and geographically than another?

Finally, some questions are a matter of judgment over appropriate strategy and cannot be answered now since they depend on the future actions of different groups within the United States and abroad.

- Will a more aggressive U.S. trade policy likely result in a mutual reduction in government intervention in the international economy, an escalation in nationalistically motivated policies, or simply better insulation for U.S. producers from the intervention of other governments?

• Will government-management-labor cooperation result in the prompt action necessary to combat foreign intervention or will that sort of decision-making structure move too slowly?

These sample questions show that intelligent debate over the U.S. reaction to the presently evolving patterns of international competitiveness and industrial structure will require the generation of much additional factual information. To adopt successful policies in the future will also require the development of a national political consensus on appropriate economic goals — and a dose of good luck in picking U.S. policies whose effectiveness depends on future actions of many groups in the United States and abroad. The initial portion of this study focused on some of the many factual questions to be addressed and confirmed the importance of sector demand characteristics and factor supply conditions in determining broad patterns of changing competitiveness. However, as recounted in Chapter 5, the experience of specific industries and products is much more susceptible to government manipulation. No attempt is made here to prescribe a proper U.S. response to this situation, but failure to alter U.S. policy from its present course could lead to inefficient, defensive and inward-looking policies that will shut the door on many opportunities in the decade ahead.

Selected Bibliography

Bowen, Harry. *Changes in the International Pattern of Factor Abundance and the Composition of Trade*. Economic Discussion Paper 8. U.S. Department of Labor, Office of Foreign Economic Research. 1980.

Branson, William. "Trends in United States International Trade and Comparative Advantage: Analysis and Prospects." *International Economic Policy Research*. Washington: National Science Foundation. 1981.

Chakin, Sol. "Trade, Investment and Deindustrialization: Myth and Reality." *Foreign Affairs*, 60, Spring 1982, pp. 836–851.

Chenery, Hollis. *Structural Change and Development Policy*. New York: University Press. 1981.

Diebold, William. *Industrial Policy as an International Issue*. New York: McGraw Hill. 1980.

Economic Policy Council of the United Nations Association, U.S.A. *The Need for U.S. Industrial Objectives*. New York: United Nations Association. 1982.

"France—An electronics plan with global ambitions." *Business Week*, May 31, 1982, p. 39.

Franko, Lawrence. *European Industrial Policy, Past, Present and Future*. Brussels: The Conference Board of Europe. 1980.

"German Officials Drop Past Objections to Government Aid for Ailing Companies," *Wall Street Journal*, May 26, 1982.

Magaziner, Ira and Thomas Hout. *Japanese Industrial Policy*. London: Policy Studies Institute. 1980.

McCulloch, Rachel. *Research and Development as a Determinant of U.S. International Competitiveness*. Washington: National Planning Association. 1978.

Morici, Peter, Arthur J.R. Smith and Sperry Lea. *Canadian Industrial Policy*. Washington: National Planning Association. 1982.

Mutti, John. *Taxes, Subsidies and Competitiveness Internationally*. Washington: National Planning Association. 1982.

Orr, James and H. Shimada. "U.S.-Japan Comparative Study of Employment Adjustment." U.S. Department of Labor, Office of Foreign Economic Research. 1982.

"Pitfalls in France's Vast R&D Plan." *Business Week*, November 23, 1981.

Reich, Robert. "Making Industrial Policy." *Foreign Affairs*, 60, Spring 1982, pp. 852–881.

_____. "The Next American Frontier," *The Atlantic Monthly*, April 1983, p. 104.

"The Pressures Mounting over Migrant Labor." *Business Week*, May 3, 1982.

U.S. General Accounting Office. *Industrial Policy: Case Studies in the Japanese Experience*. GAO/ID-83-11. 1982.

National Planning Association

NPA is an independent, private, nonprofit, nonpolitical organization that carries on research and policy formulation in the public interest. NPA was founded during the Great Depression of the 1930s when conflicts among the major economic groups — business, labor, agriculture — threatened to paralyze national decisionmaking on the critical issues confronting American society. It was dedicated to the task of getting these diverse groups to work together to narrow areas of controversy and broaden areas of agreement and to provide on specific problems concrete programs for action planned in the best traditions of a functioning democracy. Such democratic planning, NPA believes, involves the development of effective governmental and private policies and programs not only by official agencies but also through the independent initiative and cooperation of the main private-sector groups concerned. And, to preserve and strengthen American political and economic democracy, the necessary government actions have to be consistent with, and stimulate the support of, a dynamic private sector.

NPA brings together influential and knowledgeable leaders from business, labor, agriculture, and the applied and academic professions to serve on policy committees. These committees identify emerging problems confronting the nation at home and abroad and seek to develop and agree upon policies and programs for coping with them. The research and writing for these committees are provided by NPA's professional staff and, as required, by outside experts.

In addition, NPA's professional staff undertakes research designed to provide data and ideas for policymakers and planners in government and the private sector. These activities include the preparation on a regular basis of economic and demographic projections for the national economy, regions, states, metropolitan areas, and counties; research on national goals and priorities, productivity and economic growth, welfare and dependency problems, employment and manpower needs, energy and environmental questions, and other economic and social problems confronting American society; and analyses and forecasts of changing international realities and their implications for U.S. policies. In developing its staff capabilities, NPA has increasingly emphasized two related qualifications. First is the development of the interdisciplinary knowledge required to understand the complex nature of many real-life problems. Second is the ability to bridge the gap between theoretical or highly technical research and the practical needs of policymakers and planners in government and the private sector.

All NPA reports have been authorized for publication in accordance with procedures laid down by the Board of Trustees. Such action does not imply agreement by NPA board or committee members with all that is contained therein unless such endorsement is specifically stated.

NPA Officers
and Board of Trustees

Recent NPA Publications

International Relations

Changing Patterns of U.S. Industrial Activity and Comparative Advantage, by John Mutti and Peter Morici (72 pp, 1983, $8.00), CIR #14, NPA #201.

U.S. Economic Policies Affecting Industrial Trade: A Quantitative Assessment, by Peter Morici and Laura L. Megna, assisted by Sara N. Krulwich (140 pp, March 1983, $12.00), CIR #13, NPA #200.

U.S. Foreign Aid and the National Interest, by Gordon Donald, Jr. (36 pp, January 1983, $4.00), CIR #12, NPA #199.

Trade Issues in the Mid 1980s, by Sidney Golt (112 pp, October 1982, $7.00), BN #32, NPA #198.

The Newly Industrializing Countries: Adjusting to Success, by Neil McMullen (136 pp, October 1982, $7.00), BN #31, NPA #196.

Conflicts of National Laws with International Business Activity: Issues of Extraterritoriality, by A.H. Hermann (108 pp, August 1982, $6.00), BN #30, NPA #195.

Acid Rain: An Issue in Canadian-American Relations, by John E. Carroll (100 pp, July 1982, $7.00), CAC #49, NPA #194.

Canadian Industrial Policy, by Peter Morici, Arthur J.R. Smith and Sperry Lea (116 pp, June 1982, $10.00), NPA #193.

Taxes, Subsidies and Competitiveness Internationally, by John Mutti (76 pp, January 1982, $7.00), CIR #11, NPA #191.

The Evolution of a Revolution: Peru and Its Relations with the United States, 1968–1980, by Ernest H. Preeg (76 pp, December 1981, $7.00), CIR #10, NPA #190.

Flexible Exchange Rates and International Business, by John M. Blin, Stuart I. Greenbaum and Donald P. Jacobs (112 pp, December 1981, $8.00), BN #28, NPA #184.

Improving Bilateral Consultation on Economic Issues, A Policy Statement by the Canadian-American Committee (20 pp, October 1981, $2.00), CAC #48, NPA #188.

Problems and Prospects for U.S. Agriculture in World Markets, by Timothy Josling (68 pp, September 1981, $6.00), CIR #9, NPA #183.

Industrial Innovation in the United Kingdom, Canada and the United States, by Kerry Schott (81 pp, July 1981, $5.00), BN #29, NPA #187.

Canada-United States Trade and Economic Interdependence, by Peter Morici, assisted by Laura L. Megna (64 pp, November 1980, $5.00), CUSP #8, NPA #185.

The Impact of Inflation on U.S. Productivity and International Competitiveness, by Michael J. Boskin, Mark Gertler and Charles Taylor (80 pp, September 1980, $7.00), CIR #8, NPA #182.

Economic Growth Among Industrialized Countries: Why the United States Lags, by Robert M. Dunn, Jr., assisted by Salih N. Neftci (77 pp, May 1980, $5.50), CIR #7, NPA #179.

National Issues

Distressed Workers in the Eighties, by Daniel H. Saks, NAR #1, NPA #202, Forthcoming November 1983.

The Roles of Federal, State and Local Governments in Land-Use Planning, by Richard L. Barrows (36 pp, October 1982, $3.50), NPA #197.

Preparing for the Contingency of Intense Pressure on U.S. Food-Producing Resources, by Harold F. Breimyer (28 pp, January 1982, $3.00), NPA #192.

The Breeder Reactor and Prudent Energy Planning, a Statement by the NPA Joint Policy Committee on the Breeder Reactor and Nuclear Proliferation (16 pp, October 1980, $2.00), NPA #186.

NPA Membership is $45.00 per year, tax deductible. In addition to NPA publications, members receive *Looking Ahead,* a periodical published four times a year and also available at the separate subscription price of $12.50 (individual copy price is $3.25). NPA members, upon request, may obtain a 30 percent discount on all additional purchases of NPA publications.

NPA is a qualified nonprivate, charitable organization under section 501(c)(3) of the Internal Revenue Code.

A list of publications will be provided upon request. Quantity discounts are given. Please address all orders and inquiries about publications to:

NATIONAL PLANNING ASSOCIATION
Publications Sales Office
1606 New Hampshire Avenue, N.W.
Washington, D.C. 20009
(202) 265–7685

NATIONAL PLANNING
ASSOCIATION

1606 New Hampshire Avenue, N.W.
Washington, D.C. 20009

Changing Patterns of U.S. Industrial Activity
and Comparative Advantage

CIR Report #14
NPA Report #201

$8.00

NPA Committee on
Changing International Realities